Quaff!

Quaff!

Best Wines in Australia Under $15

max allen & peter forrestal

NEW HOLLAND

First published in Australia in 2000 by
New Holland Publishers (Australia) Pty Ltd
Sydney • Auckland • London • Cape Town

14 Aquatic Drive Frenchs Forest NSW 2086 Australia
218 Lake Road Northcote Auckland New Zealand
24 Nutford Place London W1H 5DQ United Kingdom
80 McKenzie Street Cape Town 8001 South Africa

National Library of Australia
Cataloguing-in-Publication Data:

Allen, Max, 1968– .
Quaff! best wines in Australia under $15.

ISBN 1 86436 618 4.

1. Wine and wine making—Directories. I. Forrestal, Peter. II. Title.

338.4764122

Publisher: Averill Chase
Project Editor: Sophie Church
Designer: Nanette Backhouse
Printed in Australia by Griffin Press, Adelaide.

This book is typeset in 9.5/15 Candida BT and 10/14 Swiss 721 Lt BT.

About the Authors

Max Allen first fell in love with wine when visiting Australia from England. As a result, he moved to Melbourne in 1992 and proceeded to work in all areas of the wine industry, from the cellar door to the bottle shop. When he's not drinking wine, Max now spends his time writing about it. He is currently the wine columnist for *The Weekend Australian*, wine and drinks editor for *Inside Out* magazine and editor of the ground-breaking web site Wine Planet. He is also a regular contributor to *Decanter Magazine* in the UK and *Wine and Spirits* in the US. He has written several books, including the bestselling award-winner *Red and White: wine made simple*, also published by New Holland.

Peter Forrestal lives in Perth and was founding editor of *The Wine Magazine* of which he is currently the associate editor. He has worked as a freelance wine and food writer and broadcaster since 1992, is wine columnist for the *Perth Weekly* and has been the wine columnist for *The West Australian*, food and wine editor of *The Western Review*, and a contributor to *Australian Gourmet Traveller*. In addition to writing seventeen educational books, Peter is author of *A Taste of the Margaret River*, co-author of *The Western Table* and the editor of *Discover Australia: Wineries* and the *Global Encyclopedia of Wine*. Until recently he was President of the Wine Press Club of Western Australia. In 1998, Peter was the Australian recipient of the St Vincent's Day Diplôme d'Honneur from the Corporation des Vignerons de Champagne.

For Max's mum—the queen of the quaffers;
and for Peter's brothers, Paul and Bernie
Forrestal—quaffing good chaps.

Acknowledgements

A book such as this is a logistical nightmare. The organisational skills, diligence and good humour of Christine de Saint Jorre (in Perth) and Romani Benjamin and Anna Davern (in Melbourne) made this book possible.

Peter wishes to extend special thanks to Nevile Phillips for his help with organising the Perth tastings and acknowledges the camaraderie of Nevile and colleagues Mike Adonis, Ben Barraclough, Steve Charters MW, Suzanne Brocklehurst and Tonia Thornley during many hours of tasting.

Joint authorship is difficult enough without having to straddle a continent in the process. Qantas has played a significant part in the collaborative process and we are grateful to the airline and Justine Bell-Morris and Ian Gay for their support. Ruth Harrison and the Perth Parmelia Hilton have also helped bring the project to fruition.

We acknowledge the support of wine producers and wholesalers who, by making available samples of their wines, provided the foundation on which the book was constructed. Our contacts at these wine companies have been unfailingly co-operative and have frequently gone far beyond the call of duty, especially Paul Avery, Michelle Beck, Steven Brown, Camille Davidson, Damian Fischer, Annie Francis, Leigh Gilligan, Andrea Gore, Kirsty Gosse, Therese Hamblion, Jodie Hannaford, Gabor Hernadi, Sally McGill, Cameron Mackenzie, Alex McPherson, Angela Medeiros, Kylie Pollitt, Nicole Potter, Pam Prior, Paul Ryan, George Samios, Renee De Saxe, Evan Schultz, Georgi Stickels, Cherry Stowman, Joanne Walker, Julie Walker and Steve Warrick. Our thanks.

We appreciate the patience of our publisher, Averill Chase, and her confidence in the project, the clear thinking and skill of our editor, Sophie Church, and the enthusiasm of all at New Holland.

Finally, we wish to thank Sophie Allen and Elaine Forrestal for their tolerance and support, especially during the most hectic days.

CONTENTS

INTRODUCTION

There's definitely something in the air—and we're not talking about a TV series here. We're talking about the buzz that's happening out in bottle shop land about good value wine; cheap wine; bargain booze. Call it what you like, there's no doubt that this is a great time to be a wine drinker on a budget—because there's an unprecedented number of budget-priced wines available.

You may be forgiven for thinking that this is not the case. A quick glance at the headlines in newspapers or the nightly news on the telly could leave you with a distinct impression that most Australian wine is rare, expensive, trendy or hard-to-get. The wine drinker is bombarded with stories about sets of Penfold's Grange selling at auction for a record-breaking 40 squillion dollars. Or the Australian wine industry's billion-dollar exports. Or trendy boutique producers in outer Woop Woop being 'discovered' by influential American wine writers and selling their entire production (of 500 bottles) to a few collectors in San Francisco. Or the introduction of the Wine Equalisation Tax and the GST on 1 July 2000, which was predicted to result in increased wine prices (the effect has turned out to be minimal).

Seasoned consumers who cut their teeth on wine in the 1970s and 1980s will also argue that many popular wines that were once affordable have slowly crept up over the $15 price line. 'Things ain't what they used to be,' they'll say, and tell you how they used to buy Chateau Ridgydidge for two bucks a bottle 'back in the good old days'. But if you dig deeper into the newspapers, or watch the rural reports, or take a walk round your local bottle shop, we think you'll see a quite different story emerging.

For a start, Australia's national vineyard has doubled in the last decade, rising from about 60 000 hectares to over 120 000 hectares. That's an awful lot of grapes. Importantly, the vast majority of the new vineyard plantings are of 'premium' varietals—chardonnay, shiraz, cabernet and so on—rather than the lower-quality multi-purpose varieties like sultana that made up the bulk of Australia's vineyards in the past. While much of the new fruit coming off these vineyards is finding its way into export wines, there is an enormous amount also being made into larger quantities of existing brands and increasing numbers of new brands. Again, the small, new, boutique, family-owned wineries popping up across Australia at the rate of one or two a week tend to grab the media attention, but there is also a significant number of new medium-sized and very big players entering the industry.

The industry itself is also experiencing some massive consolidation, and, at the big end of town with the country's largest companies, is moving towards its stated aim of becoming a very serious player on the world wine stage. Just before this book went to press, Foster's Brewing, owners of the huge Mildara Blass wine group, spent a staggering $2 billion acquiring Beringer Estates, one of the biggest wine producers in the US. This was followed by speculation that Southcorp, Australia's largest wine company, could in turn be the target of a takeover bid by a multinational drinks company.

This may sound like dry business news to you, but it has huge ramifications for the budget-conscious drinker, as the economies of scale that come with ever-larger wine companies leads to cheaper wine. The big issue remains, of course, whether that cheaper wine will still be as good, but until now both Southcorp and BRL Hardy, for example, have been able to show conclusively that they can keep quality high, despite massive increases in quantity, and there's little reason to think that will change. You can't help feeling that there's too much at stake in the modern wine market for any of the major players to let quality slip.

All of which made us think that perhaps it was time to write a guide to wines under $15. We felt that bringing this book out just as the wine juggernaut really begins to hit its straps would prime you, the consumer, with a little bit of knowledge to help you sort out the good from the bad. Which, in turn, should make you a happier quaffer.

HOW THE WINES WERE CHOSEN

For a start, we felt that $15 was a realistic cut-off point; that most people are happy to spend up to that much and are even happier if they don't have to go over $10. (A few years ago, the wine trade would have put that figure at about $12, but recent price rises have seen it shift to $15.)

We approached every major wine company in Australia and every major distributor of smaller wineries and asked them to submit samples of their under $15 wines for tasting. In many cases, where we knew a winery had wines in this price bracket, we approached the winery directly. We extended our tastings until the beginning of September, which meant that we got to evaluate many 2000 vintage whites and 1999 reds before they hit the retail shelves (and also made our publishers, a cautious lot used to working with much longer lead times, extremely jumpy!). We realise that we may have missed a few wines, but we are confident that we have caught a huge majority of the good ones. We also expect the number of entries to increase dramatically in the next edition.

Because the authors live at opposite ends of this wide brown land (in Melbourne and Perth respectively) the logistics of tasting the wines were a little tricky, to say the least. Both authors were sent samples of all the wines and while the first round of tasting happened individually in each city, the best wines from that first round were then re-tasted by the authors together at the one location (with many frequent flyer points stacked up along the way). In most cases, then, the wines we recommend in this book have been tasted at least twice, often more.

The wines were always grouped together by style or variety, and tasted blind—that is, without the taster knowing the identity of the wine in the glass in front of him. We feel this is the only fair way to assess wine. Even the faintest hint of knowledge, like a glimpse of the label, or a peek at a distinctive bottle shape, can crowd the taster with prejudice and favour. As a result, we encountered a few surprises: wines with big reputations that tasted very ordinary; and wines we would normally be suspicious of coming up trumps on the tasting bench.

Importantly, we haven't given scores for each wine, as is popular in many wine guides, magazines and newspaper columns; there are no stars or points in here. We feel that scores can lead to laziness on behalf of the consumer; it's only through reading the notes that you can discern which of two equally-pointed but quite different wines you might like. We feel that if a wine is good enough to be recommended here, that is sufficient indication of its quality. We have, though, given awards for the best wines in the book (see pages 8–11) and, in each chapter, both authors have indicated which is their favourite wine—sometimes the authors agree, but mostly there is a difference of opinion. We have also indicated which wines offer particularly good value for money. (Refer to the key on page 7.)

We've tried to make the tasting notes as informative, easy to read and evocative as possible and have tried to keep the often confusing technical wine language to a minimum, but it does appear occasionally so there is a glossary on pages 199–213 to help make sense of the jargon.

CORK, PLASTIC AND SCREW-TOP

Just a quick word on how bottles are sealed. If you've been buying cheaper wine for a few years, you will have noticed an increasing number of bottles being sealed with plastic (rather than natural) corks. We certainly came across a large proportion of wines with plastic bungs during our tastings (especially as the plastic tends to be a bugger of a thing to get off your corkscrew after you've opened the bottle, and we were opening thousands of bottles).

Many wine producers are making the shift to plastic because cork is too unreliable. Being a natural product (the bark of an oak tree), cork is susceptible to chemical taint, which in turn can taint the wine, giving it an unpleasant, musty smell or simply dulling its flavour. Industry estimates of the proportion of wines tainted in this way run from a conservative two per cent to a worrying 10 per cent— particularly at the very cheap end of the market, where economic pressure forces producers to use lower-quality corks. Which may not sound like much, but ask yourself whether you'd be happy with two per cent of your milk being tainted, or your Coke, or your bread.

At this stage, plastic corks are an acceptable alternative in cheap wines only, for two reasons. Firstly, because people who drink cheap wine probably couldn't give a stuff what's used to seal the bottle, as long as they can open it and it tastes good (whereas 'premium' wine consumers are probably a little more fussy and still like the romance of natural cork); and secondly because plastic corks have yet to prove themselves as a good, taint-free seal over a long period of time, which isn't an issue with cheaper bottles, 99 per cent of which will be drunk within hours of being bought.

For the same reasons, some producers are also summoning up the courage to use Stelvin screw-tops—notably producers of riesling. And it is courageous because many winemakers have tried screw tops before, about 25 years ago, and were met by a very negative consumer reaction. Now, the winemakers hope, consumers are a little more knowledgeble and will accept the alternative closure. We share their confidence and welcome the change as it leads to wines with great freshness.

WHAT'S IN A NAME?

We'll repeat this later in the book wherever it's appropriate, but there has been a major change over the last ten years in the way Australian winemakers can label their wines—a change that has more impact at the quaffing everyday end of the wine market than anywhere else.

For most of the twentieth century, Australian wine was labelled generically using names that originated in Europe—so red wine was 'claret' or 'burgundy', depending on whether it was firm or soft, sparkling wine was 'champagne', sweet wine was 'sauternes' and so on. When varietal labelling became popular during the wine boom of the 1970s and 1980s—with wines labelled after their grape variety, like 'chardonnay' or 'shiraz'—the generic European names stayed on, but increasingly only at the cheaper end of the market, particularly on casks.

In 1994, however, Australia signed a bilateral trade agreement with the European Community, agreeing to phase out these old-fashioned terms. For a start, they are legally protected names in Europe, and the winemakers of Burgundy, Champagne and Sauternes were becoming increasingly (and understandably) hot under the collar about anybody else trading off their reputation.

As a result, the European names have begun to drop off Australian labels, with 'burgundy', for example, replaced by 'soft dry red' and 'chablis' by 'crisp dry white'. Some continue—port, for example, and sherry—and will stay for as long as Australian winemakers can get away with it. But the day is not far off when all frowned-upon generic labelling will disappear. Just thought you'd like to know.

HOW MUCH IS IT AND WHERE CAN I GET IT?

These are possibly the two most important questions for a wine drinker and only one of them is easy to answer.

When we asked wine companies to send in samples for this book, we clearly asked that the wines they entered should have a recommended retail price (RRP) under $15, and should be available during at least the last two months of 2000—preferably for longer.

Because of their very nature, under $15 wines tend to be produced in fairly large quantity, so we feel pretty secure about the availability issue—unless otherwise stipulated, you should be able to find most of the wines in this book at most bottle shops, fairly easily. Exceptions are self-explanatory—if a wine is only available through one retail chain or direct sales operation, we have indicated that and if it's available mostly, or exclusively, through the cellar door, we have indicated that too. (Having said that, we should also add the following example of how nothing is safe when it comes to wine availability. When we tasted the 1996 McWilliams Eden Valley Riesling in early August it had recently been released and was widely available. Then it went and won a couple of trophies at a wine show and received rave reviews in the wine press. So while we're still including it here, it may not be as easy to find as we'd like.)

Price is a trickier issue. The wine trade in Australia is a dynamic and fluctuating beast, with discounting, local retail patterns and various behind-the-scenes deals and promotions all leading to sometimes quite fluid pricing. So while we can offer the RRPs that each wine company has provided us with as a guide, you may find that the price on the shelf is different—it will usually be lower, but it may be higher.

And, finally, all wines mentioned (apart from the casks, of course), are 750ml bottles, unless otherwise specified.

LET US KNOW WHAT YOU THINK

We would love to hear from you: opinions (good and bad) on the book, your quaffing experiences, tips for bargain wines we should chase up for the next edition; anything you'd like to share. You can either email your feedback to us at quaff@iinet.net.au, fax us on (02) 9453 3077 or write to us at Quaff!, Locked Bag 516, Frenchs Forest, NSW 1640.

KEY TO SYMBOLS	
Q! Quaff! Award Winner	**M** Max's Pick
★ Best Buy	**P** Peter's Pick
	P M Peter's and Max's Pick

QUAFF! AWARDS

Because everybody's first question is always 'but which wines did you like most of all?' we've decided to dish out some awards. The wines listed here are the ones that really stood out in our tastings, both for sheer quality and exceptional value for money.

Quaff! Winery of the Year 2000

ROSEMOUNT ESTATE

With an incredible 18 wines recommended out of only 20 entered for our tastings, Rosemount once again showed that they have an uncanny ability to produce vast volumes of incredibly attractive, polished, enjoyable wine at a great price.

Quaff! Wine of the Year 2000 and
Quaff! White Wine of the Year 2000

1996 MCWILLIAMS EDEN VALLEY RIESLING

This was one of the great finds of the book—a four-year-old riesling that's beginning to pick up the glorious toasty, lime-juicy richness that we'd expect from a great Eden Valley white at twice the price. Brilliant stuff.

Quaff! Sparkling Wine of the Year 2000 and
Quaff! Best Sparkling Wine Under $10

OMNI NON VINTAGE

We can't think of another under $10 fizz that is as consistently impressive and enjoyable as this. It's got complexity, a soft creamy texture, good weight and a satisfying dry finish. Simply great for the price.

Quaff! Red Wine of the Year 2000

1999 FOX RIVER SHIRAZ CABERNET

An extremely stylish, elegant red from the Goundrey winery at Mount Barker, Western Australia. This has the vibrant, peppery, spicy, intense dark juiciness and the concentration and subtlety you'd expect in a far more expensive wine.

Quaff! Best Red Wine Under $10

We just couldn't seperate these two great value quaffing reds, so we've given both of them the gong.

2000 ROSEMOUNT ESTATE SPLIT LABEL SHIRAZ CABERNET

From the winery of the year comes the bargain red of the year. With its bright purple colour, its sweet-tasting, silky-smooth berry fruit flavours and its soft, round, juicy finish, it's sensational value. The full recommended price is $11.95, but it is widely available for under $10.

1999 MCWILLIAMS INHERITANCE SHIRAZ MERLOT

Another wine from McWilliams that delivers excellent value for money. It would be near-impossible to find another red that provides this much spicy, lively, fun-filled fruit flavour for less than $7.

Quaff! Best White Wine Under $10

2000 POET'S CORNER SEMILLON SAUVIGNON BLANC CHARDONNAY

We are seeing increasingly impressive wines appearing under the newly revitalised Poet's Corner label. This is one of the best value— a really lively, aromatic, fresh young white that epitomises the quaffing philosophy.

Quaff! Best New Label 2000

HARDYS TINTARA CELLARS

Although we think the packaging of this new range is too confusingly similar to the Hardys $35 McLaren Vale Tintara reds, we're not confused for a second about the quality of the wines in the bottle: they were simply among the best chardonnay, shiraz and cabernet we tasted for this book.

SECTION WINNERS

In many cases, both authors agreed immediately on which wine was the stand-out in its bracket. In some cases, though, the opinions differ in which case we've indicated which wine was Peter's pick and which was Max's pick.

SPARKLING WINES

SPARKLING WHITES
We both liked: Omni Non Vintage

SPARKLING REDS
We both liked: Banrock Station Sparkling Shiraz

WHITE WINES

CASK WHITES
Peter's pick: Hardys Chardonnay Reserve

Max's pick: Yalumba Traminer Reserve Selection

CHARDONNAY
Peter's pick: 1998 Seppelt Corella Ridge Chardonnay

Max's pick: 1999 Hardys Tintara Cellars Chardonnay

RIESLING
We both liked: 1996 McWilliams Eden Valley Riesling

SAUVIGNON BLANC
We both liked: 2000 Plantaganet Omrah Sauvignon Blanc

SEMILLON
Peter's pick: 1999 Tyrrell's HVD Hunter Valley Semillon

Max's pick: 2000 Peter Lehmann Barossa Valley Semillon

OTHER WHITE VARIETALS
Peter's pick: 2000 Lamont's Verdelho

Max's pick: 2000 Bleasdale Verdelho

SEMILLON SAUVIGNON BLANC BLENDS
We both liked: 2000 Cape Mentelle Georgiana

SEMILLON CHARDONNAY BLENDS
Peter's pick: 2000 Poet's Corner Semillon Sauvignon Blanc Chardonnay

Max's pick: 2000 Jacob's Creek Semillon Chardonnay

OTHER WHITE BLENDS
We both liked: 1999 Alkoomi Mount Frankland White

RED WINES

CASK REDS

Peter's pick: Banrock Station Shiraz Cabernet

Max's pick: Morris Pressings Style Dry Red

MERLOT

Peter's pick: 1998 McWilliams Barossa Valley Shiraz

Max's pick: 1998 Barossa Valley Estate Moculta Shiraz

CABERNET SAUVIGNON

We both liked: 1998 Hardys Tintara Cellars Cabernet Sauvignon

MERLOT

We both liked: 2000 Deakin Estate Merlot

OTHER RED VARIETALS

Peter's pick: 1999 Baraks Bridge Pinot Noir

Max's pick: 1999 Mirrool Creek Durif

CABERNET MERLOT BLENDS

We both liked: 1998 Gramp's Cabernet Merlot

SHIRAZ CABERNET BLENDS

We both liked: 1999 Fox River Shiraz Cabernet

OTHER RED BLENDS

We both liked: 1997 Orlando Russet Ridge Cabernet Sauvignon Shiraz Merlot

GRENACHE AND GRENACHE BLENDS

Peter's pick: 2000 Peter Lehmann Barossa Grenache

Max's pick: 2000 Rosemount Estate Split Label Grenache Shiraz

SWEET WINES AND FORTIFIEDS

SWEET WINES

Peter's pick: 2000 Paul Conti 'Fronti' Late Harvest Muscat

Max's pick: 1996 De Bortoli Windy Peak Spatlese Riesling

VERY SWEET WINES

Peter's pick: 1998 John James McWilliam Late Harvest Semillon

Max's pick: 1997 Gramps Botrytis Semillon

PORT

Peter's pick: Penfolds Reserve Bin 421 Tawny Port

Max's pick: Hardys Whiskers Blake Tawny Port

CELLARING CHEAPER WINE

First of all, let's explode a couple of myths here:

Myth number one: all wine gets better with age. Frankly, no it doesn't. The vast majority of wine produced around the world each vintage is designed to be drunk within one or two years—at the most—when it's still got young, fresh fruit flavour and some kind of liveliness. Only a small proportion of the world's wines are made from the right grape varieties, with the loving care in the vineyard and winery that are needed to produce something that will develop more complexity and interest as it ages in the bottle.

This leads us to myth number two: cheap wines are all early-drinking, quaffing numbers and expensive wines are the ones that can age well. Sorry, wrong again. As you'll see, there are a surprising number of wines in this book—some as cheap as $8 or $9 a bottle (on discount)—that we reckon are delicious now but are also worth keeping for a while to develop more complexity.

Which leads us in turn to myth number three: you need a dark, underground cobweb-filled candlelit cellar before you can think about keeping wines. Now we wouldn't argue for a second that if you're a serious, cashed-up wine collector and you're buying the kind of big, tannic red wines that need 10 or 20 years cellaring before they reach their drinking peak, then a 'proper' cellar is a good idea. It has all the things you want for storing wine long-term: darkness, fairly high humidity (so the corks don't dry out), a cool, constant temperature and stillness. But we're not talking about long-term cellaring here. We're talking—and this is the crucial thing to understand—about short-term cellaring: keeping quaffing wine for six months, a year, maybe two, to try and glean a little more enjoyment from each bottle. So all you have to do is try and match as many of the ideal cellar criteria as possible, but not worry too much if you can't. We've seen all manner of cellaring options that do an adequate job: a cupboard that's been hastily insulated; under the bed in cardboard wine boxes wrapped in blankets; stashed in drawers in an old dresser in the coolest room in the house.

Let us give you a couple of examples of the benefits of short-term cellaring:

- The 1997 vintage of Mitchelton's Blackwood Park riesling was on special when it was released in 1997 for less than $10 a bottle. Only three years later, and after being stored in less than ideal conditions, a bottle opened recently is drinking brilliantly. Many other Australian rieslings and semillons at this price point would follow the same pattern.

- When Southcorp released their Thirsty Fish sparkling red wine ($13) in late 1999 it was brash, up-front and unbalanced. After just seven or eight months in the bottle, it has mellowed to a much better, rounder, more balanced drink.

- Most of the 1998 Queen Adelaide Regency Red ($7) would have been drunk by now, which is a shame, because we found in our tastings that, thanks to the quality of the fruit from the superior 1998 vintage, the wine has picked up some complexity and interest that we reckon it wouldn't have had as a youngster (and we admit that this surprised us, based on past tastings of the wine).

We're not suggesting that each of these wines will always cellar well every vintage, but they're examples of how stashing booze in a dark place can yield great benefits for the bargain hunter.

If you are interested in short-term cellaring, here are some tips to bear in mind:

- Store wines lying on their sides, so that the cork remains moist. If the cork dries out, it can let wine leak from the bottle and air leak in—a process which will eventually turn your precious drop into vinegar.

- If you want to keep white wines, buy riesling or semillon; most under $15 Australian chardonnay, sauvignon blanc, verdelho and white blends are best drunk soon after release. There are always exceptions and we've indicated these in each chapter. (In fact, we could explode another myth here, that red wines age better than whites, by suggesting that Australian riesling and semillon are better bets for cellaring than Australian reds.)

- If you want to keep red wines, think about oak-matured, fuller-bodied reds (shiraz, cabernet, shiraz cabernet blends) rather than lighter-bodied, un-oaked reds (pinot noir, merlot, grenache, etc.). Again, there are some exceptions.

- When choosing your wine storage location, try to avoid somewhere with extreme fluctuations of temperature; cold-to-hot, hot-to-cold temperature swings that will ruin a wine faster than a constant not-so-cool environment.

After saying all that, though, remember that you are the ultimate judge: you may find that you simply don't like wines with bottle age; that you relish the youthful, lively freshness of a one-year-old red. In which case, you've saved yourself a lot of bother.

TIPS FOR THE BARGAIN HUNTER

As a wine consumer, you have two choices: you can either sit back and let the wine shops seduce you into buying this week's unbeatable special, through their advertising and their promotions and their smooth talking; or you can make a little bit of effort and discover your own specials all by yourself. Here are a few tips to help you become a well-informed, quick-thinking, quick-quaffing wine bargain explorer.

READ, READ, READ

Yeah, we know the old saying 'don't believe everything you read', but in the cause of finding good value, we reckon you should take notice of at least some of the many thousands of words published about wine in newspapers, magazines and over the internet each week (but, as wine writers, we would say that, wouldn't we?).

Despite the fact that most wine columnists tend to favour stories about the more expensive, rarer, boutiquey-end of the wine spectrum, we have noticed a shift in recent times towards more consumer-oriented, value-focused articles. Indeed, in the two weeks before this book went to press, we saw at least three big stories on best wines under $15 published by major metropolitan newspapers.

The best reading you can do, though, is not necessarily product-oriented guides: knowledge equals power, and gaining knowledge about how wines are made, where they come from, why they taste different and what foods go well with them will help you become a more discerning consumer (then again, we would say that, too, wouldn't we?).

MAKE FRIENDS WITH YOUR BOTTLE SHOP

One of the best things you can do is make a nuisance of yourself at your local bottle shop. Make sure the people behind the counter know you're interested in wine and are looking out for bargains. If they're doing their job properly, they should nurture you as a valued customer—you buying cheap wine on a regular basis is just as important as one-off sales of expensive grog to people who'll never come back. In Victoria, particularly, bottle shops have often been a source of good value cleanskin wines (unlabelled bottles) and although we recommend this as a good way of coming across bargains, we would also recommend you always try before you buy, if you can (a piece of advice that applies right across the board, actually).

BUY BY THE DOZEN

In the short term, buying wines by the case, or dozen bottles, can be a real pain in the back pocket. But we thoroughly recommend it, as you are almost guaranteed to receive a discount. Indeed, this book would have been much, much bigger if we'd included all those $15.95 and $16.45 wines that are regularly discounted below $15 when bought by the dozen. If you can't afford it yourself, get together with a group of mates and each chip in the cost of a couple of bottles—that way you spread the cost but share the benefits.

GET UP AND GO

No amount of reading beats experience. Most Australians live a few hours' drive from a wine region. There's no excuse, then, not to get in the car and visit a couple of cellar doors. Here you'll (hopefully) get an idea of how to taste wine for maximum enjoyment and you'll be able to (hopefully) learn about how grapes are grown. Cellar doors are also great places to find discounted wines (bargain bins, ends of vintage, reduced to clear) and it's often possible to taste before you buy. Many wineries also have mailing lists that you can join and offer exclusive bargains to mailing list members. If you can't visit a cellar door, then many wine shops have in-store tastings, and wine exhibitions are enjoying increasing popularity.

DON'T FOLLOW FASHION

By reading and talking to people in the wine trade or the industry, you'll soon find out what's hot and what's not. You'll also learn that what's hot is usually priced according to demand (which means it's expensive) but because something's not hot, that doesn't mean it's not good (which means it's good value). You'll see what we think is under-rated throughout the book—semillon, for example, shiraz cabernet blends and fortifieds are all sources of great bargains, simply because they're not all that fashionable. Some wine regions, too, are more fashionable than others: the big, warm, inland irrigated regions of the Riverland, Sunraysia and Riverina are nowhere near as revered as, say, the Barossa or Hunter valleys, but are often much better places to find great value quaffing wine.

JOIN THE CLUB

There are disadvantages to joining a direct-selling wine club like Cellarmasters or The Wine Society—the main ones being the inability to try before you buy and the usual requirement that wine must be purchased in dozen lots. The same applies to buying wine over the internet. But we think the advantages outweigh the negative sides— look, for example, at the quality and exceptional value of the wines we have been able to recommend from the two groups just mentioned. It's a good option for the serious bargain hunter, as is the internet wine retail scene, which is still in its early, formative, highly competitive stage of development, and can be a source of incredible bargains (disclosure of interest: Max Allen is editor of the Wine Planet web site, Australia's leading on-line wine retailer).

GET OBSESSED

This is probably the only time you'll read this in a book dedicated to finding the most enjoyment for the least expense, but a big tip is to try and spend a little bit more on wine than you did last time (within reason, of course, and without plunging yourself into debt...although we can talk). If you're used to spending $6, try a $9.95 bottle of the same variety or style next time you visit the bottle shop; if $10 is your usual spend, lash out on a $14.95 bottle. You may very well think that the extra money isn't worth it, in which case revert to the old favourites and save yourself some cash. But you may also find that the slightly pricier wines can offer better value for money—in other words, by increasing your spend by 20 per cent, you can increase your enjoyment by 100 per cent. You won't know, though, unless you try for yourself.

ALL THAT GLITTERS IS NOT NECESSARILY GOLD

Don't believe the hype. Australian wine marketing departments are incredibly clever at attaching little shiny round stickers to their labels that look uncannily like medals won at some wine show or other. Don't be fooled; read the shiny stickers carefully. If they tell you the wine has won two bronze medals, it means it was judged to be fair to average quality on two separate occasions. If they tell you the winery was judged Winery of the Year at some international drinks fair in Finland in 1986, be cautious. And even if they tell you that the wine in the bottle has won a string of gold medals and trophies, while you can be safe that the wine is well-made that's no guarantee you will like it. Again—and again, again—try before you buy, if you can.

MATCHING WINE WITH FOOD:

A Load of Old Rubbish or a Heap of Fun?

Rules are there to be broken, but general guidelines are worth bearing in mind. This is the approach we take when it comes to matching food and wine: if you get too hung up on getting everything 'right' and going by the rules, you're letting yourself in for a whole heap of stress and bother. If, however, you keep one eye on commonsense but let your tongue run riot, taking pleasure out of the act of eating and drinking rather than worrying about whether they are going together perfectly, you'll probably have a better time.

In Europe, where drinking wine is considered a normal part of everyday living and is seen by most as just as important to a meal as good bread, the wine styles and traditional foods of each area have developed together over the centuries and tend to be well suited to each other.

Wine drinking (and good food) is a much more recent phenomenon in Australia, so although some distinctive wines styles have developed—Barossa shiraz, Clare riesling, Coonawarra cabernet—examples of distinctive and complementary foods are less well established. As a result, the whole idea of matching food and wine has become—or should be—a lot less rigid than in Europe. It's fun; it's not a big deal. What the hell—drink what you like with whatever you like, who cares?

Having said that, there are some wine and food combinations that are truly disgusting: big, rich shiraz and oysters; heavily wooded chardonnay with hot Asian chilli noodles; heavy, rich chocolate pudding and crisp, delicate, dry riesling. (Don't believe us? Just try them...) There are also some guidelines that are worth bearing in mind if for no other reason than they may help you to have more fun (it's all good old commonsense, really, most of it):

- Match the weight, flavour and intensity of the food with that of the wine. If you're eating something light, fresh and delicate, try and match it with something equally light, fresh and delicate. If you're eating something sweet, try and drink something that's at least as sweet. (See what we mean? Commonsense.)

- Just as the order of courses in a meal (starter, main, dessert) is determined by what tastes best (who wants to eat pan-fried salmon after a sticky toffee pudding?) so the order in which we drink wines depends on which tastes best after what. Most of us would not enjoy the finesse, delicacy and crisp acidity of a fresh young riesling if we were drinking it after the bold flavours and substantial tannins of a cabernet sauvignon.

- Look for harmony between food and wine. One of the reasons red wine goes so well with red meat is that the protein in the meat softens the firm tannin in the wine when the two meet in your mouth. Likewise, young, zesty, unwooded white wines are great with oily fish dishes because the acid in the wine helps cut through the fat of the food on your tongue.

- If possible, look for some link between the food and the wine—using the same wine you're going to drink in a sauce or marinade, for example, or drinking a wine from the same part of the world as the food (West Australian scallops and West Australian dry whites; Hunter Valley shiraz and Hunter Valley beef). Even if there's no scientific reason why the food and wine go together, it makes for a nice romantic story.

Above all, though, when it comes to matching food and wine, choose wines that make you happy. Sounds simple, really, doesn't it? That's because it is.

THE
WINES

SPARKLING
WINES

SPARKLING WHITES

Australian wine drinkers are particularly lucky people. The quality of sparkling wines available to us in the under $15 price bracket is very impressive. This is an area where the technological expertise of the wine industry in this country really shines. For some time, it has been possible to produce large volumes of sparkling wines economically in the irrigated areas along the Murray River, but, in the last decade, the quality has improved dramatically as lesser grape varieties, such as gordo, sultana and muscat, have been replanted with the 'classic' varieties—especially chardonnay and pinot noir—which are particularly suited to sparkling winemaking. As our tastings have shown, even semillon and chenin blanc make quality quaffing bubblies in these regions.

The sparkling wine market has grown steadily over the past decade, with production up just over three per cent in volume terms to more than 31 million litres each year. Led by brands such as Banrock Station and Jacob's Creek, Australian exports of sparkling wine are now worth more than $50 million yearly.

From our tasting of more than 50 bubblies, we are happy to recommend 17 sparkling wines—with at least half selling for under $10 (depending on how savage the discount is). We looked for wines that were fresh and lively with a soft, creamy texture and a finish that was crisp and dry with gentle acidity. Sugar is added in liqueur form to sparkling wine just before it is bottled and this serves to soften the acidity. When a wine is neatly balanced, this addition is subliminal: add too much sugar and the wine appears overly sweet; too little and the acid can appear fierce or searing. We marked such wines down.

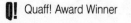 Quaff! Award Winner   Best Buy   Max's Pick   Peter's Pick

**Andrew Garrett Brut
Non Vintage
Pinot Noir Chardonnay
$14.95**

Here is a bubbly that has received deluxe treatment for its price. Winemaker Charles Hargrave has sourced chardonnay and pinot noir from cool climate vineyards and matured the wine for 12 months on its lees in the bottle before being disgorged. Older reserves (about 30 per cent of the total volume) and some parcels, which have been softened by malolactic fermentation, have been added to the final blend. The Andrew Garrett Brut has a pinkish tinge, is soft, round and full-flavoured with a creamy texture and a pleasant, gentle finish.

**Banrock Station
Sparkling Chardonnay
$12.50**

Take a single classic variety (chardonnay) from the warm, irrigated South Australian Riverland and make a good wine in significant volume. Not an easy task, but BRL Hardy have managed it. The wine goes through malolactic fermentation in stainless steel tanks before bottling which gives it additional softness and encourages the development of some savoury characters. The Banrock Station Sparkling Chardonnay is light-bodied and fine, with biscuity aromas, clean, fresh, lemony flavours and powerful, crisp acidity on the finish.

**Carrington Blush
Special Cuvée
Non Vintage
$5.95**

This is an attractive rosé style made from grapes which include chenin blanc and colombard. To give the wine its delightful salmon-pink colour a small amount of red wine is added before secondary fermentation takes place. The wine has perfumed strawberry aromas, is soft and round with a gentle, creamy mouthfeel. It is full-flavoured and has some sweetness on the mid-palate which is balanced by the crisp acidity of the finish. At the price, you can celebrate as often as you like— although picnics and barbecues are the best place for this style.

1999 Carrington Brut Reserve
$5.95

This is a big, toasty style, quite broad and full-flavoured and at its best with food. Orlando are able to keep the price down by making 150 000 cases of Carrington Brut predominantly from the less fashionable grape varieties: chenin blanc and colombard from the Riverland and Sunraysia. It is bold bubbly with powerful lemon–citrus flavours and just a touch of attractive mushroom-like flavours. The finish shows strong acidity, is fresh, crisp and surprisingly drinkable.

Cockatoo Ridge Non Vintage Brut
☆ **$10.99**

This is a big, bold sparkling wine made from semillon and chardonnay with some pinot noir which has been allowed enough skin contact to give it a faint pink tinge. It has strong, toasty perfumes and powerful lemon–citrus flavours. Bottle fermentation, some time on lees and a judicious touch of sugar has given this wine enough softness and creaminess to produce a more appealing finish than many bubblies in this price bracket.

Great Western Brut Reserve
⭐ **$9.95**

This is one of the grand old names of Australian sparkling wine, which still looks very good for the price. At present, it is a blend of semillon, colombard, grenache and chenin blanc. The red variety, grenache, is treated in the same way as pinot noir in sparkling wine: it is crushed and immediately drained off the skins leaving clear, white juice. This is a very clean, fresh, well-made and balanced bubbly with floral perfumes, intense, bready, biscuity flavours and quite strong but refreshing acidity. It's always a pleasant surprise to find a bubbly of this finesse and flavour for under $10.

1997 Killawarra Pinot Noir Chardonnay $14.00

One of the few vintage sparkling wines in this price bracket made by the traditional method (which means it undergoes its secondary fermentation in the bottle and is then matured for 12 months before being disgorged and made ready for sale). It is a blend of pinot noir and chardonnay sourced primarily from Padthaway, Coonawarra and the Barossa Valley. This is a powerful, full-bodied bubbly with bready, yeasty aromas, bold toasty, citrusy flavours, a creamy mousse and strong, bracing acidity on the finish. Best with food.

1993 McWilliams John James McWilliam Chardonnay Pinot Noir $14.00

Here is a one-off bargain: a wine that's unlikely to be repeated as the price has only dropped to below $15 to clear stocks. This is a classy blend of chardonnay and pinot noir from the premium cool climate regions of the Eden Valley and Adelaide Hills. It has some lifted citrus perfumes on the nose, is soft, round and creamy on the mid-palate, has a steely structure, plenty of power and a green apple zing to finish. This is a serious bubbly which is still youthful at seven years of age.

Moondah Maritime Sparkling White
⭐ $10.99

Western Australian bubblies are pretty rare—especially in this price bracket. So too are sparkling wines made from 100 per cent chenin blanc—the dominant grape in Houghton's popular White Burgundy. Chenin is the key variety in the highly regarded sparkling wines of France's Loire Valley—those from Vouvray, Saumur and Anjou. Ed Carr has played on chenin's high acidity, full flavour and ability to handle sweetness to make the Moondah bubbly. It has some fruity, almost tropical aromas, is round, soft and quite sweet with grassy mid-palate characters, strong acidity and sweetness on the finish. For those who prefer a sweet style.

Omni Non Vintage
0! P M $9.95

This was the best of the batch, value-wise, our favourite bubbly of this book and one of BRL Hardy sparkling winemaker Ed Carr's most impressive achievements. He might get more kudos for his ultra-premium Arras ($50) but making a bubbly in large volumes as consistently good as Omni takes our breath away. Made from chardonnay and pinot noir and aged on lees for 9–12 months, this has some bready, yeasty aromas, apple and pear flavours and gentle lemony acidity. It has a soft creamy texture, good weight, and a satisfying dry finish. Simply outstanding for the price.

Seaview Brut
$8.40

Currently the largest selling sparkling wine in Australia, Seaview Brut is a blend of pinot noir, muscadelle, chenin blanc and semillon grown in a range of South Australian vineyards. It has some light lemon–citrus perfumes, is quite neutral in flavour and finishes dry and crisply acidic. Some may find it too crisp and even sharp on the finish, but if this style of bubbly suits, you'll love the price.

Seppelt 2000 Brut
Cuvée
$9.95

This is an impressive bubbly which is made from non-classic sparkling wine varieties such as sauvignon blanc, riesling and white frontignac. It has toasty, sherberty aromas and apple, pear and lemon flavours and is intense, tight and powerful. There is some creaminess on the palate and a crisp, refreshing acidity on the finish. Subliminal sweetness softens it nicely. Named to remind you of the millennium rather than to suggest that the grapes came from the most recent vintage. Great value.

Seppelt Fleur de Lys Pinot Noir Chardonnay $13.00

Made predominantly from chardonnay and pinot noir from premium Seppelt vineyards in Padthaway, Great Western, Drumborg and Barooga, this is a top quality, non-vintage sparkling wine that is fermented in the bottle. It is fresh and clean with some lemony–citrus and apple characters, is quite robust and powerful with attractive full-flavour and a crisp, bracing acidity.

Sir James Cuvée Brut $14.95

When it comes to making sparkling wines, BRL Hardys Ed Carr has the Midas touch. This is a non-vintage blend of chardonnay and pinot noir, which is grown in three cool regions: the Yarra Valley, King Valley and Padthaway. The Sir James Brut has lemon–citrus aromas, is light-bodied, soft and round and has an almost creamy texture with a touch of sweetness to make it more approachable. We both enjoyed it because it was fine, clean and fresh.

Tatachilla Pinot Noir $14.95

This classy bubbly is made entirely from hand-picked pinot noir, which is sourced from Tatachilla's premium Clarendon vineyard in McLaren Vale. Because pinot is a red grape it needs to be treated particularly carefully in the winery to avoid picking up anything but a tinge of colour. Instead of being put through the crusher, whole bunches are gently squeezed in a high-tech Bucher sparkling wine press. The wine picks up a touch of salmon-pink colour from contact with the skins of the red grapes and some strawberry characters. This is a subtle sparkler with a creamy texture and a gentle but lively finish. Excellent value.

Wolf Blass Brut Non Vintage $14.00

This is made from chardonnay and semillon sourced from a range of vineyards in South Australia and Victoria. The wine is given an average of 12 months on lees before it is disgorged. A small amount of reserve wine, which has been aged for three years, is added to the blend to improve its complexity. The Wolf Blass Brut is a bracing style with bold, appley fruit and powerful acidity that is clean, crisp and refreshing.

Yellowglen Yellow $12.00

This top-selling non-vintage wine contains fruit from both the 1995 and 1996 vintages, sourced from many parts of south-eastern Australia, including a significant amount of pinot noir, chardonnay and semillon from the premium regions of the Barossa Valley, McLaren Vale and Coonawarra. The Yellow has some sweet bubble gum, confectionery and lemony characters on the nose and on the palate. Although it's fairly sweet, soft and round, it's still crisp and refreshing on the finish.

classic quaffers

GREAT WESTERN BUBBLY

It's all too easy to be seduced by the history and romance at Seppelt's Great Western winery. There are the endless cool, dark tunnels (known as the drives) dug out of the soft rock by unemployed gold miners when the winery was established by Joseph Best in the 1870s. There are the old enamelled Victorian-era advertising signs used by Best's successor, Hans Irvine, when he expanded the winery and vineyards in the 1890s and made Great Western wines famous around the world. And there are the huge trademark palm trees planted by the Seppelt family when they bought the place from Irvine in 1918. The place is saturated in history.

But that's not what we're interested in here (as romantic as it is). What we're interested in is one of Australia's best-loved bargain sparkling wines: Seppelt Great Western. Three hundred thousand cases are churned out each year from the huge, ultra-modern winery that sits above the drives and is now the sparkling winemaking facility for all Southcorp's fizz brands (Seppelt, Seaview, Killawarra, Minchinbury and so on) together amounting to two million cases annually.

The name Great Western was first used on a sparkling wine label by Irvine in the 1890s (the name comes from the town of Great Western where the winery is situated, which itself was named after a ship that brought many settlers to Australia). Benno Seppelt continued to use it as a distinctive brand name from the 1920s onwards, and by the early 1960s, Seppelt Great Western was one of the three big names in Australian 'champagne'.

According to Seppelt's chief winemaker Ian McKenzie, Great Western 'champagnes' from that period routinely won trophies and medals in wine shows and were mostly made from a now almost-extinct grape variety called ondenc, or Irvine's white, grown at Great Western and at Seppelt's pioneering new cool-climate vineyards at Drumborg in far south-west Victoria.

'Over the following years, though, the price pressure from cheaper brands such as Orlando and Minchinbury forced us to use cheaper grapes like sultana from the warmer Riverland districts,' recalls McKenzie. 'The 1970s were a bit of a low point for the brand and my challenge in 1983, when I took over, was to lift the standard of Seppelt Great Western fizz.'

Today, the blend for the Great Western sparkling wines—the dry Brut Reserve and slightly sweeter Imperial Reserve—is roughly one third sultana from the irrigated regions, picked early to provide one good, clean, crisp, neutral flavour base; one third premium white grapes like colombard, semillon and chenin blanc to provide fruit flavour; and one third 'blanc de noirs' (white juice pressed from black grapes, like grenache or shiraz) to provide body and fullness.

There have been other changes. About three years ago, the wine switched from being fermented in the bottle (a fairly costly and time-consuming way of producing bubbles) to being fermented in a tank. Market research had told McKenzie that loyal Great Western customers neither knew nor cared about the differences between the two processes—all they cared about (quite rightly) was the quality and the price. As he suspected, nobody noticed.

And about nine years ago, Great Western became one of the first popular Australian sparkling wines to lose the word 'champagne' from its label. Again, nobody noticed. Seppelt Great Western had become synonymous with reliable fizz for generations of Australians. It simply didn't need to hide behind a French name any longer.

SPARKLING REDS

This is a unique Aussie style which has a strong local following. It does tend to polarise opinion: you either cherish it with a passion, or hate it with undisguised ferocity. We are unashamed lovers of traditional sparkling reds and are delighted that the field for our tastings, while small, was very impressive. Of the 11 bubblies tasted, we have reviewed five—a terrific strike rate.

Sparkling reds are made in the same way as sparkling white. However, there are two key differences. With sparkling whites, the winemaker is looking for slightly under-ripe, quite neutrally flavoured base wine. The best sparkling reds are made from base wines that are ripe and rich with concentrated flavours. The blend will be improved if some components of it have a bit of age, as this will give the finished bubbly more character.

After the yeast from the secondary fermentation is removed from the bottle or tank, sugar is added in liqueur form just prior to bottling. Because of the need to soften its acidity and strong tannins, significantly more sugar is added to the wine. When this is done carefully, so that the fruit, tannins and sugar are in balance, the sweetness will be barely noticeable.

 Quaff! Award Winner ★ Best Buy   Max's Pick   Peter's Pick

Banrock Station Sparkling Shiraz
P M ⭐ $10.95

A sparkling quinella for Ed Carr and BRL Hardy with this little ripper, as they add our award for Best Sparkling Red to their gong for Best Sparkling White. Making a non-vintage wine allows Carr to blend some older, softer, richer shiraz with vibrant, fresh young material to give this bubbly a touch of complexity. Max loved its 'rich, round generosity and leathery characters', while Peter enjoyed, 'the sweet vanillin oak and mulberry aromas, its soft, velvety texture and the balance between sweetness and the gentle tannins on the finish'.

Cockatoo Black Sparkling Red
$14.50

The Cockatoo Black is a non-vintage blend of cabernet sauvignon, shiraz and merlot that has made a big impact on this segment of the sparkling red market with its first couple of releases. As the base wine is aged in old French oak for 12 months, it becomes softer and more complex when transformed into a sparkling red. The dominance of cabernet in this blend produces a big, brooding style, vibrant and powerful with smokey, briary aromas and deep, rich, concen-trated blackberry flavours.

Killawarra Sparkling Shiraz Cabernet
$14.60

This is a bold, full-flavoured classic Australian sparkling red that is sourced from some of South Australia's premium areas, including Langhorne Creek, Padthaway, the Barossa and Eden Valley. The base wine (including about 30 per cent of older reserves) is stored in large, old oak casks before being blended and bottled. It is then made according to the traditional method: it goes through a secondary fermentation in the bottle, remains on its yeast lees for 12 months, is disgorged and prepared for sale. Both of us enjoyed its dense raspberry, plum and blackcurrant characters, richness and concentration, supple almost velvety mouthfeel and dry, tannic finish.

Thirsty Fish Sparkling Red $13.80

When the press release says something like, 'a contemporary new sparkling wine designed to tickle the fancy of indulgent consumers who will be drawn to the confident and decadent look of this delicious drop' we usually take evasive action. Thank goodness for blind tastings: neither of us had any idea what we were tasting and both were pleasantly surprised. The packaging may be trendy and designed to appeal to those who are young at heart, but it's a good bubbly. Made from shiraz and cabernet sauvignon, the Thirsty Fish Sparkling Red is reasonably light-bodied, has some raspberry, plum and blackcurrant flavours, a pleasing softness and enough sweetness on the finish to make it an enjoyable drink.

Yellowglen Red Non Vintage $12.00

This is a big, rich, sweet commercial style that many will find extremely attractive. It is a non-vintage blend of three harvests: 1997 (44 per cent), 1998 (30 per cent) and 1999

(26 per cent) and is sourced from South Australian regions including Padthaway and the Limestone Coast. It is a straight-forward, oaky sparkling red with attractive creamy texture and a powerful sweet finish. It reminded Max of raspberry ripple ice-cream.

WHITE
WINES

THE STORY OF THE CASK

The cask: it's such an icon of Australian quaffing. A box of cheap, cheerful white in the fridge, another box of cheap, rough red on top of the fridge, or on the kitchen bench; there's a cask at every backyard barbecue, every fly-blown picnic, every parent–teacher night and every gallery opening across the country, every day of the week. The silver bladder has been a prop at countless buck's nights and hen's parties and student raves and 'B and S' balls. There's even been an art exhibition devoted to the cask, with various creative types asked to decorate their favourite source of inspiration.

Casks are so widespread, so popular, so huge—accounting for almost half of all wine sold in Australia—that it's hard to imagine life without them. It feels like the cask has been around forever. It hasn't of course. In fact, the cask has a remarkably short history.

The first attempts to package wine in a soft, collapsible airtight container go back to 1965 when Tom Angove produced a prototype version for fortifieds at the large Angoves winery in the Riverland. The advantages of such a package over glass flagons (the most popular bulk container at the time) were clear—as you poured wine out from the bladder, it shrank, meaning there was no air coming into contact with the remaining wine, meaning it didn't go off. But Angove soon ran into the problem that would plague the development of the cask for the next ten years: it was almost impossible to make the point where the tap system met the bladder impermeable to air. In other words, the bloody things leaked like crazy.

Penfold's were the next to have a go at it in 1968, with a bladder inside a tin can and utilising a tapping device called the Airlesflo, created by Charles Malpas, a Geelong engineer-cum-back shed inventor. It was a marketing success with the public, but a technical failure—and soon led to so much ill will with the wine trade (who were sick of the bloody things leaking all over their shops) that the project was cancelled.

The demise of Penfold's involvement almost killed the idea completely. Some other producers, such as the Berri co-op in the Riverland, persisted with the idea (Ian McKenzie, now chief winemaker for Seppelt but then working for Berri, remembers hand-filling silver bladders and hanging them up around the winery to see which ones leaked before packing them) but nobody managed to crack the secret.

Then in 1971, Ray King, a newly-employed young marketing director at Wynns Winegrowers in Melbourne, convinced his boss, David Wynn, to have another look at Charles Malpas' invention. Since Penfolds' project flop, Malpas had developed his tapping system further and was successfully trialing some small volume cask packaging at Dan Murphy's Cellars in the Melbourne suburb of Prahran. King saw an opportunity to make his mark in the wine industry and put a marketing plan together for a cardboard cask.

Wynn was reluctant at first but, inspired by King's enthusiasm, agreed to invest the fairly substantial amount needed to take the idea further. Six months and a few truckloads of soggy cardboard later, the Wynvale cask was launched. In typically confident Wynns fashion, the company assured the trade that all the old problems had been solved and the brand became a huge hit, soon outselling Wynns' own successful flagons. (Ray King won a Hoover marketing award for his work on the Wynvale cask and went on to become the CEO of Mildara Blass—ironically the only large Australian wine company not to produce cask wines.)

Although Wynns secured a three year exclusive with Malpas' tapping system—ensuring them, they thought, dominance of this new cask wine market—it wasn't long before both Lindemans and Orlando also came out with their own casks, using the Scholle bag-in-box system, developed in the US in the 1940s (some would say rather appropriately) for packing battery acid. And just over ten years later, the cask accounted for half of Australia's wine sales.

While there's no doubt that the cask has had an enormous impact on turning Australia into a wine-drinking nation, and has been a quiet driving force behind much technological and industry progress, it hasn't all been plain sailing. The incredibly low cost of cask wine—to a great extent a result of wine being taxed on its value and not its alcoholic volume—has contributed, you could argue, to many cases of destructive alcohol abuse. In the past, there has also been much concern over the levels of preservatives used in cask wines (which by their nature are more prone to oxidation and spoilage). And during the mid-1990s, when low-yielding vintages led to an acute shortage of grapes in Australia, much of the local cask wine market was filled by cheap—and generally sub-standard—imported wine from Spain, Chile and the south of France.

Working on this story, and tasting our way through most of Australia's casks, we found that the preservatives and imported wine blending issues are today less of a problem—the sulphur dioxide levels in most of the wines seem to be acceptable, certainly from a sensory point of view, and most of the wines we tasted are predominantly sourced from within Australia. However, arguments over the inequitable taxation, accessibility and low cost of cask wine—and its adverse impact on the community—are still very much with us. And they still haven't quite solved the impermeability problem either. Casks are not indestructible; they will not protect a wine forever. In fact, those who work at the bulk end of the industry recommend drinking cask wines no more than nine months after packing—and seeing as every cask has to have a packing date printed on it by law, this is a piece of advice we would heartily endorse.

CASK WHITES

The good news is that the overall standard of Australian white wines sold in casks is pretty good. Certainly, most of the wines we tasted were well-made with very few suffering from winemaking faults. We were looking for wines that were clean, fresh, bright and had immediate appeal—and we found quite a few that fitted that description. Any that were over-sulphured, stale or oxidised were marked down.

The bad news is that the sweetest styles (generally labelled moselle, fruity lexia or soft fruity white) were disappointing—bad news because this is the largest segment of the market. Of the 35 tasted in this category, only five were considered worthy of review. The vast majority were overly sweet, without the underlying acidity to prevent them tasting syrupy and cloying.

The increase in consumption of wine in the past decade has seen a rise of almost 40 per cent in white wines sold in bottles and a drop of about five per cent in cask whites. However, white cask wines still represent about 50 per cent of all table wines sold in Australia (and red casks only about six per cent) and so, by any reckoning, it's a major segment of the market.

We think that the often quite misleading terminology used in the packaging of casks is a matter that deserves urgent attention by wine producers and legislators. The use of protected European names is set to disappear from our casks—riesling will not be used after the end of 2000, for example—but although Australia has agreed to phase out names such as chablis, lambrusco, moselle and white burgundy, no date has been set for this to occur. Very few producers seem to be taking any meaningful steps to create new terms and descriptions to replace the old names.

In the meantime, the terms currently used to describe casks have no legal definition and you simply can't rely on the words to give you a clue: we found many crisp, dry whites that would be more appropriate labelled as fruity medium whites, moselle or even fruity lexia. It's open slather for the producers and it's the consumer who is left to guess at the style of wine they are buying.

As a result of the tasting, we've arrived at some general tips for buying white cask wines:

- small casks contain better quality wine and represent better value;
- casks labelled with varietal names, such as chardonnay, chenin blanc, sauvignon blanc and traminer, tend to be better than those with generic labels such as fresh, dry white, classic dry white, soft, fruity white or medium dry white, or with protected European names such as chablis, moselle or riesling;
- the best white cask wines are produced from the chardonnay grape.

All casks are 4 litres unless otherwise specified. And while some are actually more than $15, their equivalent 750ml bottle price is much lower than $15, so we felt they were worthy of inclusion.

Q! Quaff! Award Winner   ★ Best Buy   **M** Max's Pick   **P** Peter's Pick

drier styles

**De Bortoli Semillon
Trebianno Chardonnay
$14.95**

Our favourite of the De Bortoli casks. We enjoyed its soft, easy-drinking, dry style and attractive fleshy texture.

**Hardys Chardonnay
Reserve (3 litres)
P $16.95**

An appealing style with apple and honey characters and a slight oakiness but with youthful, direct, chardonnay flavour. This is lively and fresh, soft and round and delightfully fleshy. As Max summed it up, 'a good, honest Aussie Charders.'

**McWilliams Colombard
Chardonnay Premium
Selection (2 litres)
$10.95**

This is a pleasant, flavoursome white with some straw and tropical fruit characters and a fresh, dry finish.

**Morris Chablis
$11.95**

Here is a crisp, fresh and clean wine with a pulpy, white grape flavour, a fleshy texture and a satisfying dry finish—just what you would expect from this style.

**1999 Morris
Chardonnay Reserve
$16.95**

Delightfully ripe with apple and tropical fruit flavours, it is soft, round and fleshy and has plenty of body. Max loved its 'crisp drinkability'.

**1999 Yalumba
Chardonnay Reserve
Selection (2 litres)
$14.95**

Here's a wine to appeal to lovers of fuller chardonnays. It has a full, fruity nose and ripe flavours that are almost too peachy but with some liveliness and a clean, dry finish. Richer, softer and fleshier than other chardonnay casks.

Yalumba Chenin Blanc Reserve Selection (2 litres) $14.95

There was some variation between the casks we tried at separate tastings, with Max obviously tasting the better cask and enjoying the wine for its fresh, clean, slightly herbaceous zing.

1999 Yalumba Traminer Reserve Selection (2 litres) M $14.95

One of the highlights of our tastings. It has a beautiful, spicy perfume and typical traminer varietal character on the nose and on the palate. Much better flavour definition than most cask wines. Soft, round and seductive yet clean and fresh. A delight.

Yalumba Unwooded Chardonnay Limited Release (2 litres) $14.95

A pleasant wine with a good lemony, fruit flavour, it is lively, clean and has a crisp, dry finish. A refreshing drop.

sweeter styles

Coolabah Fruity White Wine Reduced Alcohol $9.95

Removing the alcohol almost invariably takes away most of the flavour from a wine but this is a better example than most. The wine has some lifted, fruity aromas, is soft, fresh, clean and sweet without being cloying.

Kaiser Stuhl Soft Fruity White Moselle $12.00

Enticing muscat aromas and bold, grapey characters. This is a sweet, flavoursome wine that has a better acid balance than most cask wines of this style, and so is less unrelievedly cloying on the finish. 'A triumph,' said Peter.

Lindemans Cellar Choice Soft Fruity White Moselle $14.00

The muscat variety gives sweet wines like this a distinctive, grapey flavour and allows them to stick out from the pack. This is soft and fruity but with a clever balance between the grapey sweetness and crisp acidity.

Renmano Frontignac Chenin (2 litres) $9.95

This is a well-made white in the sweeter style which manages to convey a sense of fun. Lively perfumes of spice and confectionery and some fat, grapey flavours. It is soft and sweet on the palate and has distinct musk-like flavour. A wine you'll remember.

Sunnyvale Medium Dry White $7.90

This is a cleverly made wine that delivers a well-made, straight-up-and-down white featuring grapey, muscaty perfumes, a soft, fleshy texture and sweet lolly-water flavours with huge popular appeal. If you are looking for a fruity, sweet quaffer at a good price, you'll be well pleased with this.

CHARDONNAY

There were more chardonnay grapes picked across Australia last year than any other wine grape variety, white or red—a whopping 210 000 tonnes (okay, so the sultana crop was 250 000 tonnes, but we don't count that because only 110 000 tonnes were used for winemaking). Incredibly, though, winemakers are still clamouring for more. Despite many reports to the contrary in the wine press, there is no chardonnay glut and people are not bored with the grape. Wine drinkers both here and overseas can't seem to get enough of the stuff.

Even more incredibly, chardonnay has grown from a few tonnes picked from a handful of vineyards to Australia's most plentiful wine in just 30 years. Before winemakers like Murray Tyrrell in the Hunter Valley and David and Adam Wynn in the Eden Valley began playing with commercial quantities of the grape in the early 1970s, Australia's premium white wine market was dominated by riesling and semillon.

During this period, the style of Australian chardonnay has swung like a pendulum as winemakers have experimented with fermenting in oak, malolactic fermentation and sourcing grapes from different vineyards. At its extremes, chardonnay in this country has moved from the big, fat, buttery barrel-fermented warm-climate styles of the 1980s to the lean, anaemic, delicate unwooded styles of the 1990s. More recently, though, the better examples have managed to find a middle ground by combining the power and richness of the grape with more subtle winemaking techniques. Nowhere is this middle ground more important than in the under $15 sector of the market.

On the face of it, the fact that we have recommended over 40 chardonnays seems encouraging—it's good, surely, that there are so many fine examples of the grape around. But you have to weigh that up against the fact that we had to taste close to 200 chardonnays to find 40 we liked. This is not because 160 of the wines we tasted were badly made—indeed, outright winemaking faults were, as you'd expect, few and far between. It was because too many of the 160 wines we haven't recommended were boring: bland, unexciting and coarse. So while we love the fresh, ripe approachability of good Aussie chardonnay—especially if it's under $10—we also can't help feeling that there's still too much wine out there which is using residual sweetness and clumsy winemaking (heavy-handed oak chips, unbalanced malolactic creaminess) to hide the fact that overcropping and stretching produces dull, dilute flavours.

A couple of things to bear in mind before you dive in. First, when we use the word sweetness in these tasting notes, we are usually referring to fruit sweetness rather than sugar sweetness—a ripe fullness of flavour, rather than a real sweetness on the tongue. All of these wines would technically be referred to as 'dry'. (But having said that, it is not uncommon for many of these wines to contain just a touch of residual sugar and this is not necessarily a bad thing if done well.) Secondly, we've split the chardonnays into three groups: unwooded, wooded under $12 and wooded over $12, to break the list up a little and to help you, the consumer, find what you're looking for.

 Quaff! Award Winner   Best Buy   M Max's Pick   Peter's Pick

unwooded styles

2000 Chapel Hill Unwooded Chardonnay $13.95

Chapel Hill winemaker Pam Dunsford has always produced one of the best unwooded chardonnays in the country, ever since the winery launched the style in the mid-1990s. It's a blend of McLaren Vale and other South Australian regions and while it has (at this young stage) very attractive, lifted, almost floral aromas, it's refreshingly dry, crisp and lean in the mouth. Great with seafood and simple salads.

2000 De Bortoli Gulf Station Unwooded Chardonnay $14.95

De Bortoli have grown over the last 10 years to become one of the Yarra Valley's largest producers, with many ranges of wines on offer. The mid-priced Gulf Station range offers great value and this terrifically vibrant young unwooded chardonnay is one of the best wines in the line-up. Reflecting its cool-climate origins, it has very fragrant, perfumed, almost passionfruity intensity, with a fruit-sweet but very zingy, crisp flavour in the mouth. Nice wine that deserves to be drunk young and fresh.

2000 Evans and Tate Gnangara Unwooded Chardonnay $12.45

While we find many of the Evans and Tate red wines (both under and over $15) to have dipped in quality over the last couple of years, we were very impressed with the winery's unwooded whites in our tastings (see also the Margaret River Classic recommendation in the semillon blends chapter, p.103). This terrific young chardonnay has been sourced from Margaret River and other wine regions and is almost as pungently aromatic as a good sauvignon blanc, with passionfruit flavours and delicate but intense, zesty juiciness in the mouth.

2000 Hugo McLaren Vale Unwooded Chardonnay $14.50

This wine, from small McLaren Vale producer Hugo Wines, is very much in the light, fresh, uncomplicated style of unwooded chardonnay. It's very crisp, very refreshing, very zesty, but it lacks any strongly identifiable fruit character. There is, of course, nothing necessarily wrong with that—sometimes all you want is a glass of crisp, dry white wine, and you can't be bothered having to negotiate with too much flavour. If so, try this.

2000 Normans Unwooded Chardonnay $12.00

For some reason, Normans have given this $12 wine a label of its own, rather than package it up with the White Label range of slightly more expensive wines. We reckon they could probably get away with charging more for it, because it's a lovely, ripe, satisfying drink, with lots of sweet round yellow fruit and a balancing lick of citrussy acidity. (Not that we want the price to go up, just that we think it's good value.)

2000 Yalumba Unwooded Chardonnay ☆ $10.95

This is possibly the best argument for drinking unwooded chardonnay young that we've ever tasted. An incredibly lively, crisp, perfumed wine with almost grassy aromas and a really refreshing green apple liveliness running through it. Sensational value—especially if you can find it discounted to under $10.

2000 Taylors Promised Land Unwooded Chardonnay $13.95

This has been a surprisingly good wine for a few vintages now—surprising because the Clare Valley isn't the first place that springs to mind when you think of Australia's better chardonnay regions. It's not overly ripe or rich, but instead is very much in the crisp, almost neutral, refreshing dry white wine mould. A good value, reliable seafood wine.

2000 Wolf Blass Unwooded Chardonnay $13.95

Wolf Blass, the celebrity winemaker who rose to fame by producing big, oaky red wines and whose motto during the 1970s and 1980s was 'no wood, no good' must have been livid when told an unwooded chardonnay was to appear under his name. Even though it's not in the traditional Wolf Blass style (or perhaps because of it), this is still a lovely drink— a little sweet in the mouth, but there's plenty of lifted, herbaceous, fresh fruit flavour to keep it lively and crisp.

oaked chardonnay under $12

1999 Bleasedale Winemakers Selection Chardonnay $11.95

Langhorne Creek, where the historic Bleasedale winery is located, is witnessing massive vineyard expansion at the moment, as many of the country's large wine companies learn to appreciate the region's warm climate and relatively abundant water supply. The big companies are also coming because of the ripe, generous, soft flavours the region produces in wines like this: a really comfortable, fruit-sweet, round and gently oaky chardonnay.

Available through Cellarmasters: call 1800 500 260, or visit www.cellarmasters.com.au

1998 Bulletin Place Chardonnay $11.00

The Bulletin Place range of wines is named after the restaurant run during the 1970s by noted wine personality, author and wit, Len Evans. The brand is designed to offer good value drinking across a range of styles. We found the chardonnay to be the best wine in the range, with heaps of up-front ripe yellow fruit flavour and equal amounts of toasty, spicy oak. An appealing if obvious style.

2000 Charles Sturt University Chardonnay $11.95

Charles Sturt Uni near Wagga Wagga in southern New South Wales has a popular and highly respected winemaking course, with a fully-equipped commercial winery on site, and has been selling wines under its own label for a number of years. When we tasted it, we found this wine to be incredibly youthful, with very crisp, sweet aromatic fruit not quite integrated with smoky oak characters. By the time you taste it, though, we expect these two elements to have come together.

1999 Cockatoo Ridge Chardonnay
☆ $10.99

We found the Cockatoo Ridge range to be a fairly reliable source of good value, easy-drinking wines. The brand was started by Geoff Merrill, one of McLaren Vale's great winemaking characters, and is now a huge seller for distributors Tucker Seabrook. We liked this chardonnay, with its good balance between ripe, round peachy fruit and sweet, creamy butterscotch and vanilla flavours. Very well made.

1999 Cottlers Bridge Chardonnay
☆ $6.45

This would have to be one of the biggest bargains in the book. It's from Casella Wines, one of the Riverina's increasing number of interesting, quality conscious producers. We liked it because it has ripe, citrussy, peachy chardonnay fruit flavours in perfect balance with just enough vanillin toasty oak flavours to add interest without going over the top. Seriously good value.

1999 Deakin Estate Chardonnay
$9.95

You know where you are with Deakin Estate. This Murray River regional brand continues to go from strength to strength and almost every time we taste the wines we can see why: the formula is just so spot-on, as in this chardonnay. Well-made and full of easy-drinking, sunshiney fruit flavour it's a wine that offers reliable, simple enjoyment.

1999 Haselgrove Sovereign Chardonnay $10.95

We found the range of wines under the Haselgrove Sovereign label were characterised by an appealing, immediate ripe fruitiness. This wine is no exception, exhibiting the peachy, round, fresh fruit flavours typical of McLaren Vale, where most of the grapes are sourced. We also like the fact that it is unencumbered by the kind of heavy-handed, unsubtle oak characters that can spoil too many chardonnays in this price range.

2000 Houghton Chardonnay $10.95

Like many of the Western Australian white wines reviewed in this book, this chardonnay seems to exhibit more of a regional character than a varietal character. On first sniff, you could almost be forgiven for thinking this is a sauvignon blanc, with its pungent, ripe, passionfruity aromas. But then, in the mouth, the rich, round, mellow flavours of chardonnay kick in, finishing soft and full. A white wine packed to the gills with sunshiney flavour.

2000 Jacob's Creek Chardonnay $8.95

The chardonnay produced under the Jacob's Creek label has improved enormously over the last few years and the new 2000 vintage wine is a good example of that improvement. It's got juicy, relatively restrained, lemony peachy fruit flavours balanced by a soft, creamy oak character. Not incredibly complex or demanding, and very much a drink-young proposition.

1999 Jindalee Chardonnay ☆ $11.50

In just two short years, Jindalee has established itself as a fairly major new name in the crowded field of value wine producers located around Mildura in north-west Victoria. While we weren't impressed by all the Jindalee wines, we certainly liked this very easy-drinking chardonnay, with its full, luscious, ripe tropical fruit and soft background of creamy oak. A full, drink-now style. Very good value.

1997 Leo Buring Clare Valley Chardonnay ☆ $11.95

Like the 1998 Leo Buring semillon, which we also recommend, this wine benefits from being undervalued and unrecognised (both the Clare Valley and the Leo Buring name are better known for riesling). A couple of years ageing in the bottle have resulted in a wine with really seductive, full toasty oak characters and rich, pineappley fruit. We can't help feeling the price reflects Southcorp's desire to quit this vintage and move on to the 1998. We are only too happy to oblige.

1999 McWilliams Hanwood Chardonnay $9.95

There is fierce competition in the under-$10 chardonnay market in Australia, and one of the strongest contenders out there fighting the battle at the moment is this wine from McWilliams. Interestingly, not only is it knockin' 'em dead in bottle shops and restaurants, but it's also wooing the judges in wine competitions: this vintage is a multi-gold-medal winner, and the 2000 vintage (to be released soon) won top gold at this year's

Brisbane Wine Show. It's not hard to see why—it has surprising complexity, stylish, spicy oak flavour and vibrant sweet crisp fruit.

1999 Penola Estate Coonawarra Chardonnay ☆ $10.20

Exceptional value chardonnay from Coonawarra, bottled exclusively for the Liquorland group. It's a fragrant, aromatic white wine, with juicy, lean fruit flavours complemented by quite rich, soft oak. Normally thought of as a red wine region, Coonawarra is not exactly renowned for its chardonnay—especially under $15— but this and a couple of other recommended wines on these pages may help to change that perception. **Available through Liquorland and Vintage Cellars.**

1999 Poet's Corner PC Chardonnay $11.95

The Poet's Corner label has been revitalised over the last couple of years and turned into a funky, bold-coloured brand aimed at the younger, groovier drinker. But unlike some other 'groovy' young brands, the wine in the bottle is often very good. This is Mudgee chardonnay at its most full-flavoured and generous, with ripe, melon and peach fruit propped up by lots of toasty oak. Not terribly subtle, but lots of bang for your buck.

2000 Salisbury Estate Chardonnay $8.95

Salisbury, once the excellent value label of Mildura-based Alambie Wines, is now part of the same stable of wines that includes Cranswick Estate and

Haselgrove. It's still reliably good value, though, if this wine is anything to go by. Very ripe, aromatic style of chardonnay, all up-front pungent tropical fruit only just held in check by some noticeably crisp acidity.

1999 Saltram Classic Chardonnay
⭐ **$9.95**

Precisely what we'd expect to taste in an everyday drinking chardonnay from a traditional Barossa winery like Saltram— a ripe, round, yellow wine, with full, soft, pleasing pineappley fruit flavour. Good, honest drinking at a good, honest price.

2000 Yalumba Oxford Landing Chardonnay
$7.99

Although Yalumba make much of their rich heritage in the Barossa Valley, they rely heavily on grapes from the much larger inland irrigated region of South Australia's Riverland to produce wines in the great value Oxford Landing range. This is a delightful, youthful, zesty young chardonnay with light, lifted citrussy, almost sherbety fruit flavours and lots of drink-me-young appeal.

2000 Lindemans Bin 65 Chardonnay
⭐ **$8.70**

It's become a boringly repetitive question that gets asked each year, but honestly, how do Lindemans manage to make such a good, correct, fun, satisfying drink at this quantity and price? An annual production of close to two million cases of wine this good almost defies belief. It's the archetypal cheap Aussie chardonnay: a great balancing act between rich, ripe peachy fruit, spicy vanilla oak and lemony acidity. Very impressive. Very drinkable.

oaked chardonnay over $12

**1999 Andrew Garrett
Chardonnay
$14.50**

The Andrew Garrett winery in McLaren Vale founded its reputation during the 1980s and 1990s on big, bold, popular reds (like the reds we also recommend elsewhere in the book). Now under the ownership of Mildara Blass, we can also recommend this label as a good source of surprisingly refined, restrained, subtle, dry and savoury chardonnay.

**1999 Annies Lane Clare
Valley Chardonnay
$14.95**

This is simply a terrific chardonnay, made from premium Clare Valley fruit—although it's already quite developed and forward and we wouldn't recommend keeping it for too much longer. It's a full-bodied white wine, with a rich and creamy palate supporting bold, oaky flavours of buttered toast and melon. Drink with full-flavoured fish dishes like Mediterranean seafood stew.

**1999 Cowra Estate
Cricketers Classic Bat
Chardonnay
$14.50**

Once you get past the very daggy, gimmicky label (we thought it made the wine look more like a $6 bottle than a $14 bottle) you find a quite delicious chardonnay, showing all the vibrant, fresh, green apple and citrus fruit flavour that Cowra, in central New South Wales, is famous for. By far the best and most interesting wine among the entries from Cowra Estate that we tasted for this book.

1999 Deakin Estate Select Chardonnay $13.00

The Select range has recently been launched by Deakin Estate to replace the slightly more expensive Alfred premium range. It's interesting to compare this with the 'standard' Deakin chardonnay—it's got a similar background of ripe, full, peachy fruit, but the foreground is filled with much more obvious and seductive toasty oak and butterscotchy, creamy savoury flavours. Big, happy chardonnay. Drink now with full-flavoured chicken dishes.

1999 Hardys Tintara Cellars Chardonnay M $14.50

A new label from Hardys, designed to commemorate the company's old McLaren Vale winery and vineyards, and not to be confused (although we can see how you could) with the more expensive Tintara red wines (a shiraz and a grenache) which are packaged in much more expensive distinctive bottles with an etched logo. This is a blend of McLaren Vale and Adelaide Hills fruit and has lots of lovely, ripe flavour and lemony sweetness, but is balanced by some well-handled savoury oak flavours. A very stylish chardonnay at the price.

1999 Jamiesons Run Chardonnay $14.95

The successful Jamiesons Run brand was kicked off by a red (which is also recommended in the other red blends chapter, p.169) and has been joined over the years by other varietals, including this chardonnay. It reflects the cooler climate of Coonawarra with its tight, refreshing citrus fruit flavours and juicy palate, balanced by some good tangy, savoury oak and a nice, lingering finish.

2000 Kangarilla Road McLaren Vale Chardonnay $14.00

Considering much of the chardonnay from McLaren Vale can be quite full and tropical-fruity, we were impressed with how this small winery has managed to produce such a crisp, lively, bright-tasting white wine and release it so soon after vintage. Predominantly unwooded, with a portion of barrel-matured fruit to give it depth, it's a very aromatic, sweet chardonnay with heaps of juicy, refreshing appeal.

1999 Lysander Chardonnay $14.95

This excellent chardonnay is from the relatively new and relatively cool region of Mount Benson on the southern South Australian coast, roughly parallel with Coonawarra. It's a very stylish wine, with prominent but seductive toasty, biscuity oak flavours wrapped around a core of creamy, citrussy fruit. In fact, we were so impressed that we questioned whether it was indeed under $15 and were told that although strictly speaking its RRP is $15.95, it is regularly discounted to $14.95—so there you go. Available through Cellarmasters: call 1800 500 260 or visit www.cellarmasters.com.au

1998 Morris Chardonnay $12.95

One of two white wines to have impressed us from Morris, a name normally associated with reds and fortifieds. Considering the warmth of the Rutherglen region—which you would expect to produce big, rich wines—this is a surprisingly subtle, restrained chardonnay. It has a leanness and youthful freshness, balanced by hints of honey and lemon tang. A dry, savoury style that could benefit from a few years' bottle age.

1999 Neil McGuigan First Estate Chardonnay
⭐ **$12.95**

Neil McGuigan is one of the Hunter Valley's finest winemakers and has recently moved from the small Briar Ridge winery to head up the large Rothbury Estate. This wine was made for Cellarmasters using Hunter Valley and Mudgee fruit and while it reflects those two regions' rich, ripe fruit characters (tropical, pineappley flavours), it's deliciously crisp, fine and lively, with very subtle, unobtrusive oak flavours. Available through Cellarmasters: call 1800 500 260 or visit www.cellarmasters.com.au

1999 Preece Chardonnay
$14.95

We found the high-volume, well-known, distinctive second label from central Victorian winery Mitchelton to be an inconsistent source of good drinking: some wines in the range are fairly ordinary, while some are excellent. This is one of the better ones. It reflects its cooler climate origins (half the fruit came from the King Valley in north-east Victoria), because although it has some toasty savoury oak and intense yellow fruit flavour, it is restrained, on the lighter side and refreshing.

2000 Rosemount Estate Diamond Label Chardonnay $14.95

We could almost—almost—have recommended this wine without tasting it. Few other Australian chardonnays are so consistently good, year in, year out. Few others have so consistently impressed critics from Melbourne to New York. As it happened, though, the wine also shone in our blind tastings, with its fragrant, seductive, ripe, almost tropical fruit flavours, its crisp, melon-like fruit juiciness on the palate and its well-judged use of subtle oak.

1998 Seppelt Corella Ridge Chardonnay P $14.00

Along with the 'Sheoak Spring' Riesling (which we have also recommended, see p. 77), this is one of two wines to thankfully come in under the $15 mark in Seppelt's excellent range of Victorian regional blends (the reds in the line-up—Harpers Range Cabernet and Chalambar Shiraz—are also very good, but are just over $15). It's a lovely chardonnay for the price, with quite full, tangy nectarine and citrus fruit balanced by creamy, lingering flavours of wheatmealy oak. Very good mouthful of white wine.

1999 Sir James Chardonnay $13.95

Yet another good chardonnay from the BRL Hardy stable, named after the larger-than-life former head of the company, Sir James Hardy. It's a blend of fruit from two of South Australia's premium cool-climate regions and has lovely, lifted, aromatic yellow fruit characters, a good crisp palate and deliciously enticing toasty oak flavours from its partial barrel fermentation. It finishes clean and dry. Excellent value.

1999 Tony Bilson Selection Mount Benson Chardonnay $14.95

Although we might well challenge the rather outrageous claim on the back label that Tony Bilson 'stands unchallenged as Australia's greatest chef', we're not going to argue with anyone over the high quality of this wine (Bilson has a range of wines bottled for him by Cellarmasters, of which this was the only one we can recommend). It is uncannily similar in style and quality to the Lysander Chardonnay mentioned on p.62 (another Cellarmasters chardonnay sourced from Mount Benson) with prominent but seductive toasty, biscuity oak flavours wrapped around a core of creamy, citrussy fruit.
Available through Cellarmasters: call 1800 500 260 or visit www.cellarmasters.com.au

1999 Westend Three Bridges Chardonnay $14.95

Westend is one of an increasing number of wineries in the huge irrigated Riverina (and Murray River) districts to be concentrating on raising their quality image. The Three Bridges range is where you'll find Westend's top wines (there is also a sensational Three Bridges cabernet sauvignon, which has a full RRP of $18.95, but may be available in some bottle shops for close to $15). We'd love to see more Riverina chardonnay like this produced on a regular basis—it's got heaps of ripe, sweet, citrussy fruit flavour, but also has admirable intensity, restraint and a great crisp finish.

1999 Yalumba Barossa Chardonnay $14.95

The Yalumba name has been associated with the Barossa Valley for 150 years, so it's not surprising to find that the winery has some longstanding and very valuable relationships with some of the region's best grape-growers. These growers are the key to the quality of this wine, with its juicy white grapey flavours and well-judged, lightly handled oak. A stylish, correct chardonnay that could age quite well for a year or two in bottle.

LINDEMANS BIN 65 CHARDONNAY

The scale of Lindemans Bin 65 Chardonnay boggles the mind. This year, from the 2000 vintage, Lindemans produced a staggering 18 million litres—or 24 million bottles—of their world-famous brand. Trying to get your head around that much wine is hard enough, but reconciling the quantity produced with how good the stuff tastes is almost impossible. Just try for a second to imagine 18 million litres of wine: enough to fill a respectable football stadium to overflowing (well, maybe not, but it would have to be close).

Lindemans Bin 65 is one of Australia's real success stories—one of the driving forces behind the export boom of the last decade. Since the first vintage in 1985, the wine, with its distinctive orange label, has achieved incredible success overseas—it is exported to 57 countries; in the UK it is the number-one-selling Australian chardonnay; and in the US it's the top-selling imported wine, featuring as a 'Best Buy' in the influential magazine *The Wine Spectator* no fewer than 11 times.

It's not all export glory, though. Australia still accounts for one third of the wine's sales each year—indeed, it's the third highest-selling white wine after Queen Adelaide chardonnay and Houghton White Burgundy. It's still eight bucks a bottle, and it's still a remarkably good wine.

In May this year, while the tail-end of the 2000 vintage still rumbled away in the cooler parts of the country, Max travelled to the vast Lindemans Karadoc winery near Mildura in north-west Victoria to taste a mere 100 of over 200 individual wines that went into this year's

Bin 65 blend. It was a fascinating glimpse into the logistical nightmare that is the making of this wine. It was also a tasting packed with mind-numbing figures.

Chardonnay grapes were sourced from 25 different regions across south-eastern Australia this year. Over half the fruit came from the hot, inland irrigated areas of Sunraysia and the Riverland (one huge single vineyard near the Karadoc winery alone contributes 5000 tonnes of grapes, the equivalent of about three million litres of wine) but the rest came from a surprisingly diverse collection of areas including the Barossa and Clare valleys in South Australia and the cool, premium districts of the Yarra Valley and the Strathbogies in Victoria.

Most of these components make up less than one per cent of the final blend, but each is crucial to the overall quality and complexity of the wine. The idea—palate-teasingly illustrated by tasting the 100 wines—is that a small proportion of cooler-climate, premium quality wine, with its delicate flavours and crisp acidity, is there to balance and lift the rich, fat, soft, generous backbone of warmer-climate wine in the blend.

Seven Southcorp-owned wineries in three states were used to process all this fruit (Southcorp is the parent company of Lindemans), with the final assembly and bottling taking place at Karadoc. Because of the sheer quantity involved, the wine is assembled and bottled in stages throughout the year, pretty much on demand, with the right proportions of each component being trucked to Karadoc and blended up in big tanks according to the master recipe. We usually make a point of avoiding the obligatory tour of the bottling line in big wineries (working on the 'seen-one-seen-'em-all' principle), but at Karadoc the super-fast line is a must-see: it fills and packs 20 000 bottles every hour and runs 24 hours a day.

A dedicated team of people in vineyards and wineries across the country are responsible for the logistical side of Bin 65, but responsibility for the reliability, quality and style are all pretty much down to one man: Lindemans' chief winemaker, Phillip John. John is meticulous, almost to the point of obsession, and is totally devoted to his work. Although a fairly reticent and shy man, if you get him on to the subject of flocculating yeast he becomes animated; get him on to the subject of Bin 65 and you can barely shut him up. Ensuring that the first bottle of Bin 65 to rush off the bottling line is every bit as good as the 24 millionth is a challenge that he takes very personally.

It has to be worth it, though. Just knowing that every one-and-a-half seconds someone somewhere in the world is opening a bottle of Bin 65, pouring themselves a glass and smiling, must make Phillip John and his team of winemakers immeasurably proud.

RIESLING

Riesling is the ultimate quaffing wine. It's a big call, we know, but we can't think of another grape variety that offers so much drinking excitement for less than $15. Just look at the list of wines we recommend here—at least half a dozen of them would be considered by many to be among the very best rieslings in the country, regardless of price.

Australia's classic riesling regions (Clare and Eden valleys in South Australia, central Victoria, and Great Southern in Western Australia) dominated our tastings, so when you drink many of these wines you're drinking the product of a specific place (which may or may not be important to you). We would confidently recommend stashing away almost every single one of these wines in a dark, cool place for at least five and up to 10 years, safe in the knowledge that they will develop more complexity and richness—even two or three years in less than ideal cellaring conditions may reap rewards.

So why is riesling so underrated? It has a lot to do with the fact that, until the end of this year, the name riesling has been allowed on labels as a generic term for aromatic, medium dry white. The cask doesn't have to contain a drop of varietal riesling. No wonder people had a poor image of the grape. That's beginning to change, though, with rieslings from top producers like Grosset and Petaluma finally breaking the $20 barrier (a recognition of their desirability). But while the rieslings at the cheaper end are beginning to see some price rises as a result, they're still, on the whole, incredibly affordable.

Ironically, just as Australians turn to riesling once again, the 2000 vintage conditions resulted in sometimes dramatically reduced crops in some of the best regions for the grape—particularly Clare and the Barossa. So while we rave about the quality of the 2000 rieslings from these areas, we're afraid there may not be as much of them to go around as we'd like.

 **Q!** Quaff! Award Winner ★ Best Buy **M** Max's Pick **P** Peter's Pick

2000 Annies Lane Clare Valley Riesling
$14.95

Sourced predominantly from the Annies Lane vineyard in the Polish Hill River region, just to the east of Clare, this has been shaping up over the last few vintages as one of the region's most reliable rieslings. It's got everything you want from a young Clare riesling: excellent zesty, youthful lime-juicy drinkability and a crisp, refreshing, intensely flavoured finish. There is possibly no better match for fresh Asian influenced fish salads than a young riesling like this.

1999 Cellarmasters Rare Print Series Eden Valley Riesling
$14.95

The Cellarmasters premium Rare Print series of wines is notable for two things: the stylishly old-fashioned, slightly European packaging (the labels feature an old nineteenth century food-related engraving—hence the name); and the quality of some of the wines that have been released. This riesling is a welcome addition to the range, with an austerity and restraint that we associate with the variety when it's grown in the Eden Valley —there are enticing hints of citrus and blossom, but it's mostly about a very dry, crisp, lean palate. Will age well. Available through Cellarmasters: call 1800 500 260 or visit www.cellarmasters.com.au

1999 Chateau Tahbilk Goulburn Valley Riesling
$14.95

From one of Australia's oldest operating wineries in the Goulburn Valley in central Victoria. Even though it's less than two years old, this lovely riesling seems to be already picking up some bottle-aged characters, with a slightly deeper yellow colour and rich toast and lime flavours creeping in to accompany the fresh juiciness. However, we're not worried. Past experience of drinking older bottles of this wine lead us to think that it may develop quite quickly but then hold for a few years more after that—a 1989 tried recently was still superb. Note that from the 2000 vintage, the winery's name will change to simple, plain old Tahbilk.

2000 Eaglehawk Riesling
⭐ **$12.95**

A multi-district blend that often offers more approachable, immediate pleasure than some of the other rieslings produced under the Wolf Blass label, which, while very good, can take time to evolve (Eaglehawk is one of the cheaper labels in the Mildara Blass portfolio, with similar fruit sourcing and winemaking to the Wolf Blass wines). This is really full-flavoured, juicy riesling, with a touch of sweetness and plenty of almost tropical characters like pineapple and melon. Unlike many of the other Wolf Blass rieslings, we'd suggest you drink this early.

1999 Grant Burge 'Thorn' Eden Valley Riesling $14.80

The Eden Valley, up in the hills overlooking the Barossa Valley, is renowned for producing austere, dry, almost minerally rieslings that taste like sucking on river stones when they're young (honest!) but can age into glorious drinks over five to 10 years, exhibiting a core of lime juiciness. This is classic Eden Valley: we liked it precisely because it is so savoury, dry, austere and crisp, with hints of the floral juiciness but overall, lovely zesty dryness.

1999 Houghton Frankland River Riesling
$10.95

The Frankland River district in Western Australia's vast Great Southern region is thriving at the moment and although much of the new vineyard development is focusing on red grapes—particularly shiraz—there is a fair amount of interest too in riesling. Taste this excellent value wine and you'll see why: it has the herbal, lavender, floral smells and flavours typical of this part of the world (and so different from riesling grown in the eastern states), coupled with a soft, citrussy, refreshing finish. A lovely wine.

1999 Hardys Siegesdorf Riesling
$10.95

This brand enjoyed a huge reputation during the 1970s, before chardonnay stole riesling's crown (you could argue) as king of Australian white wine. It was the wine that a young Brian Croser—now head of Petaluma—made his name with. Even though the wine may not now be considered a classic, its exceptional value for money ensures it continues to be cherished by quaffers. It has plenty of citrus and lime flavour, a quite full, juicy palate and finishes nice and round and soft. An easy-drinking, all round favourite riesling.

**2000 Leasingham Bin 7
Clare Valley Riesling
$12.95**

Like the Richmond Grove rieslings also recommended and many other (more expensive) 2000 vintage Clare Valley rieslings, this wine has been released with a screw-top Stelvin cap. This is to avoid the risk of contamination from a faulty cork—a problem which is said to taint up to five per cent of all wine. The Stelvin closure has the added benefit of ensuring the wine stays ultra-fresh, which is a good thing as this wine is wonderfully crisp, lean, zesty and intense, with a steely, flinty dryness running along its spine. We also tasted the 1999 vintage and thought it was an excellent, soft, lime-juicy riesling with a good chalky dryness to the finish.

**1999 Leo Buring
Clare Valley Riesling
☆ $12.00**

The Leo Buring name has a long and highly-respected association with the Clare Valley and with riesling: famously, Leo Buring rieslings from the 1960s and 1970s are still drinking well—indeed, the best wines are still improving. For some reason, though (and a very ordinary label redesign may have something to do with it) the brand and its wines are undervalued today. All the better for bargain hunters, because it means terrifically well-made, crisp, focused, soft but refreshing rieslings like this are available for a song. Buy a dozen; drink some while it's young and lively and stash away for five years when you can enjoy its mellow, toasty flavours.

1996 McWilliams Eden Valley Riesling
◗! P M $14.95

This was one of the great finds of the book—a four-year-old beginning to pick up the glorious, toasty, lime-juicy richness that we'd expect from a great Eden Valley riesling at twice the price. Just after we tasted it in early August, it won two trophies at the Melbourne Wine Show, beating wines that really are twice the price. As a result, it's attracted a lot of attention from the wine press, and many people have discovered it's charms for themselves. We think it's a superb wine that deserves all the accolades it gets.

2000 Mitchelton Blackwood Park Riesling $13.95

One of two rieslings we're happy to recommend from the Goulburn Valley in central Victoria. At this young stage, it's a bit reticent—not overly aromatic, very dry, crisp and lean. But there's definitely some lovely, brooding, perfumed, juicy lime fruit waiting in the wings, biding its time before it can burst out from the glass and onto your tongue. We'd give it about six months, and expect that it will drink well for five years at least.

2000 Peter Lehmann Eden Valley Riesling ☆ $12.00

The Peter Lehmann image may revolve around big, beautiful Barossa reds, but we reckon the bargains are to be found in the white wines in the range, particularly the semillon and the riesling—which, not coincidentally, happen to be sourced from the slightly cooler Eden Valley. This is a simply sensational young riesling, bursting with lime juice and citrus zest flavours and with the kind of zingy, refreshing vitality in the mouth that makes you reach out for another sip, another glass. Terrific stuff, terrific value.

2000 Pewsey Vale Eden Valley Riesling ☆ $11.95

The low price of this potentially classic wine reflects a run of less than exciting vintages through the mid-1990s. The last couple of releases, though, have raised the quality level immensely and this now represents great value for money. Sourced from one high vineyard in the Eden Valley, it's an incredibly tight, focused riesling with intense floral, lemony finesse, great intensity and a steely dryness. Delicious now with seafood, it should keep happily in a dark place for five to 10 years. Very good.

2000 Richmond Grove Barossa Riesling $14.95 and 2000 Richmond Grove Watervale Riesling $14.95

The Richmond Grove rieslings are possibly the best example of how undervalued this grape variety is in Australia today. They are made by John Vickery, the undisputed king of riesling, a winemaker with decades of experience who was responsible for the classic wines put out under the Leo Buring label in the 1970s. The wines he makes are some of the purest, most exciting expressions of the grape in the country; they are bottled with Stelvin screw-top seals rather than cork to ensure a slow development in bottle (says the label) for 30 years. And yet they're available for under $15—often closer to $13, sometimes less. We're not complaining—we're just pointing out how lucky you are. As usual,

we can't decide which wine we like more—
the up-front, juicy fullness of the Barossa
wine, or the more fragrant, lime-zestiness
of the Watervale. Sensational wines,
sensational value.

**1998 Seppelt 'Sheoak
Spring' Riesling
$13.30**

This is a full-flavoured riesling sourced
primarily from a vineyard in the cool
Strathbogie Ranges, north of Melbourne.
Although we both liked the wine enough
to recommend it, we had some
disagreements over the style: Peter liked
its strongly aromatic, almost musky
aromas, while Max thought it tasted a
little flat—as though it were experiencing
the famous dip in flavour that riesling tends
to go through between fresh youth and
complex middle age. Either way, a different
style to the racy intensity of the South
Australian rieslings. Worth trying, to see
which of us you agree with!

**1999 Vintage Cellars
Clare Valley Riesling
$12.95**

This wine has got that magic combination
of regional and varietal flavours—the lime
and green juiciness of the riesling grape
at its best, plus the refreshing dry, chalky
leanness you'd expect from the Clare
Valley. Not the most sensational riesling
we tried, nor the cheapest, but its wide
availability—through Vintage Cellars
nationally—makes it well worth
recommending. As we went to press,
it was spotted at one Vintage Cellars
store for $10.
Available through Vintage Cellars.

**2000 Wynns
Coonawarra Estate
⭐$ Riesling
$10.65**

Bearing in mind that this wine is almost universally discounted to under $10; that Coonawarra didn't experience anywhere near the same low crop levels as, say, Clare during the 2000 vintage; and that Wynns riesling has a proven capacity to age in the bottle for at least a decade (we really enjoyed a 1990 recently), this would have to be a candidate for lifetime membership of the Quaffing Bargain Club. It's an excellent young riesling—crisp, juicy, floral, lime-juicy but, above all, elegant, delicate and dry to finish. Yum.

SAUVIGNON BLANC

Sauvignon blanc can be a great quaffing wine. At its best, it produces ravishingly attractive, early drinking whites: fresh, lively and with distinctive varietal character ranging from the riper tropical fruit (lychee, gooseberries and passionfruit) to the crisp, vibrant, green-tinged herbal. The best wines have crisp, dry acidity and are lovely chilled in the warmth of summer. Some are good for drinking on their own, although most are improved by being served with food—light, tangy salads, some subtle vegetarian dishes, milder, less spicy Asian dishes and delicate seafood may all be enhanced by sauvignon blanc.

Unfortunately, we found all too few sauvignons under $15 that we could describe as great quaffers. In our tastings, we saw far too many poorly made sauvignons: dilute wines that were lacking in flavour; overly sweet; without any balancing acidity; or simply ruined by winemaking faults. This is obviously a variety that is best produced in cool-climate regions, at reasonably low yields (expensive) and so, because it is usually made without oak and sold off quickly (not so expensive), it is difficult to find wines that are both cheap and of good quality. Except here.

 Quaff! Award Winner   Best Buy   M Max's Pick   Peter's Pick

**2000 Jamiesons Run
Sauvignon Blanc
$14.95**

The first vintage for this variety under the Jamiesons Run label has been sourced from cooler climes, including the Adelaide Hills and Padthaway. Made by Mildara Blass winemaker David O'Leary, it is a good example of a sauvignon blanc that sits in the herbal (rather than tropical fruit) spectrum. There are some green pea and fresh herb aromas, the wine is clean and lively on the palate, has green pea flavours and a crisp, zingy finish.

**2000 Lindemans Bin 95
Sauvignon Blanc
⭐ $8.70**

A wine like this shows the big companies at their best: Lindemans have been able to call on their vast resources of fruit from the premium regions of Padthaway (80 per cent of the wine) and Coonawarra (20 per cent) for this budget-priced drop. Concentration of flavour (which is vital to good sauvignon blanc) has been improved by lower than normal yields. This is due to frosts, poor flowering of the fruit and light winter rains during the 1999 winter, prior to harvest. The 2000 Bin 95 is the best of the cheapies we tasted: clean, fresh and well-made, reasonably concentrated melon, gooseberry and tropical fruit flavours and a short finish that is a touch sweet. At the price, though, few would complain.

**2000 Mount Trio
Sauvignon Blanc
$14.00**

This is the relatively new label of Plantagenet winemaker Gavin Berry and his wife Gill, who have a small vineyard in the Porongurups sub-region of the Great Southern. They sourced the fruit for this wine from nearby Pemberton and picked

it in two batches—the first to highlight crisp, bracing acidity and the second to bring out riper fruit characters. There are restrained tropical fruit aromas on the nose but the wine is clean, fresh and well made, and shows some grassy and tropical fruit flavours and a crisp, lively finish.
Limited availability some states.
Call (08) 9853 1136 or email mttrio@telstra.easymail.com.au

2000 Plantagenet Omrah Sauvignon Blanc
P M $14.95

Plantagenet have consistently made very good sauvignon blancs under this label for several years although this vintage is as good as any they've made. Cool to moderate temperatures and generally good weather enabled the grapes to ripen slowly and so concentrate flavours for the 2000 vintage. For this delicious white, winemakers Gavin Berry and Gordon Parker take fruit from Plantagenet's home base in the Great Southern as well as Margaret River. This represents remarkably good value for your money: a big, rich food wine with lively aromatics and delightful pungency. It shows herbal and green pea aromas, is fresh, round and fleshy, with soft, green pea flavours and gooseberry and tropical fruit characters on its lingering zesty finish.

2000 Preece Sauvignon Blanc
$14.95

Legendary winemaker Colin Preece is celebrated by this value-for-money label of the Goulburn Valley's Mitchelton Wines. Long-serving current winemaker, Don Lewis, has taken the fruit for this varietal from cool-area vineyards, mainly in the fertile King Valley with a small proportion coming from the Strathbogie Ranges in the central Victorian high country. This is a delightful expression of cool-climate sauvignon blanc with floral tropical fruit aromas, soft, round, fleshy texture, tropical fruit and lychee flavours and fresh, zingy acidity on the finish.

2000 Rosemount Diamond Label Sauvignon Blanc $14.95

Few countries allow the kind of multi-regional blending that Australia has become famous for and few companies handle the logistics involved in blending wines from different areas better than Rosemount. This wine is drawn from the company's vineyards in the Upper Hunter, the Adelaide Hills and Orange, and was made at their wineries in the McLaren Vale and Denman before being blended at Rosemount's headquarters in the Hunter. This is a lively, tangy expression of sauvignon blanc showing grassy, green apple and lemon flavours with a touch of wild herbs. It has some green pea character on the nose, is fresh and lively in the mouth and has a crisp, dry finish.

2000 Schinus Sauvignon Blanc $14.95

Consistently among the better examples of the variety at this price point, Schinus is the second label of Mornington Peninsula producer Dromana Estate. Innovative vigneron, Garry Crittenden, has produced a lively zingy sauvignon blanc that is restrained in its youth but will open up after a few months in the bottle. It has some lemony, grassy flavours and a clean, crisp finish.

**2000 Smithbrook
Sauvignon Blanc
$14.95**

Now part of the Petaluma empire, Smithbrook was a large pioneering vineyard in the Pemberton region established in the late 1980s. It made a small volume of wines under its own label but sold off most of its fruit to other companies. Revitalised since being taken over by Petaluma, Smithbrook has now released three very good sauvignon blancs under Brian Croser's direction. The 2000 Smithbrook has grassy, tropical fruit perfumes and lively passionfruit and blackcurrant leaf flavours, is fresh and light-bodied and has a clean, crisp finish. One of the best.

**2000 Westend
'Richland' Sauvignon
Blanc
$9.95**

With sales in excess of 100 000 cases, Bill Calabria's Griffith-based Westend winery is one of the smaller players in the Riverina. But the quality can be impressive even with its budget-priced 'Richland' label. One of the very few wines at this price point with distinctive, sauvignon blanc character, some herbal notes on the nose, clean, fresh and light-bodied green pea and herbal flavours and a crisp, dryish finish.

SEMILLON

What an exciting, encouraging and delicious bunch of wines this turned out to be! The numbers alone tell you heaps about what an excellent quaffing option Australian semillon is—from approximately 35 wines tasted, we can heartily recommend 16. Sure, we can recommend more chardonnays (about 40) but we had to taste our way through over 200 wines to find that many. The fact that semillon's strike rate was so high indicates two things to us: that the grape variety is well-suited to warm Australian wine-growing conditions; and that the variety is incredibly undervalued. In fact, we'd even go so far as to say that semillon is, on the whole, a more reliable and more interesting source of fuller-bodied, dry white wine bargain drinking than chardonnay—so there you go!

What impressed us about the best semillons was their distinctive varietal and regional flavours—fairly difficult characters to find consistently in wines under $15. We liked the fact that the best young Hunter whites tasted like Hunter Valley semillon: unwooded, low in alcohol (10–12 per cent), fresh, chalky and slightly herbaceous. We liked the fact that the best wines from the Barossa Valley were gloriously different: oak-matured, lemony, toasty, higher in alcohol (12–13.5 per cent) and richer than the Hunter wines.

And we loved the fact that—because semillon is so undervalued and under-rated—there are a couple of wines out there which have been left to linger, unloved, on bottle shop shelves for a year or two after their release and which have, by default, picked up complex, bottle-age characters (the exception being the classic Mount Pleasant Elizabeth from the Hunter Valley which isn't even released until it's four years old). This is where Australian semillon's greatness lies: in its ability to improve in the bottle.

 Quaff! Award Winner ⭐ Best Buy Ⓜ Max's Pick Ⓟ Peter's Pick

**1997 Brown Brothers
King Valley Semillon
$14.95**

North-east Victorian winery Brown Brothers isn't the first name that springs to mind when you think of good semillon, but this delicious three-year-old wine has corrected that misconception. Thanks to its bottle age and some judicious, subtle oak maturation, the wine has developed really quite seductive, complex, toasty, smoky aromas and a rich, golden, crisp-finishing flavour of lemons and just a touch more toast. Drink now, while it's at its peak.

**1999 Cellarmasters
Rare Print Series
Barossa Valley Semillon
$13.95**

This is another of the Rare Print Series to come up well in our tastings. We are impressed that Cellarmasters have matched the quality of the wine in the bottle with stylish packaging. The nineteenth-century engraving is the centrepiece of a distinctive and elegant label and this Barossa Semillon is right up to the mark too. It's been partially fermented and aged in barrel, but the intense, youthful lemon and lanolin-flavoured semillon fruit has soaked up all the oak and resulted in a tight, crisp white wine. It's good now, but should develop more richness and complexity over the next five years.
**Available through Cellarmasters:
call 1800 500 260 or visit
www.cellarmasters.com.au**

**1997 Distinguished
Vineyard Series Hunter
Valley Semillon
$11.25**

What a bargain! This classic, aged semillon comes from a single vineyard in Pokolbin (in the heart of the Hunter Valley) which is owned and tended by a family of respected local grape-growers, the Howards. When the wine was released a couple of years ago, we remember thinking that it would age well and were amazed to find it still for sale. We're not complaining for a second, though—this wine is a great combination of rich-smelling, toasty lemon aromas followed by the classic regional lightness, crispness and cleanness in the mouth. A lovely, delicate, dry white wine at a great price.

Available through Vintage Cellars.

1998 Gramps Barossa Valley Semillon $14.95

One of the most generously-flavoured, full-bodied semillons in the tasting, this is a fabulously complex wine for the price, with aromas of freshly-buttered toast and wood smoke swirling around a core of soft, rich, ripe yellow fruit. Wonderful with garlic roasted chicken, it's a white wine you wouldn't want to drink too cold—the colder it is, the more you'd dull that complexity. And even though it has benefited from a year or so in bottle—making it more interesting than when it was released—we wouldn't want to keep it much longer.

1999 Grant Burge Barossa Vines Semillon ☆$ $11.50

Unlike its big barrel-aged sister (Zerk Barossa Valley Semillon), this cheaper Barossa semillon is fermented in stainless steel tanks and has a fantastic freshness and liveliness. There are green apple and green pea flavours and some of semillon's trademark lanolin characters. The wine finishes with a delicious twist of lemony citrus, which we associate with the variety when it's grown in the Barossa.

1999 Grant Burge Zerk Barossa Valley Semillon
$14.80

Made using semillon grapes sourced from Robert and Janine Zerk's Lyndoch Valley vineyard, this is a full, soft semillon with classic Barossa characters. The ripe semillon fruit gives the wine wonderfully lifted, tangy, spicy, crisp lemon flavours, while the partial fermentation in oak barrels has added a honeyed roundness to the mouthfeel. Drinking really well now, it should pick up more richness over the next year or so.

1998 James Busby Oak Matured Barossa Semillon
$12.55

Another good semillon from the Barossa winery of Grant Burge, but this time bottled exclusively for Liquorland and sold under the James Busby label. In many ways, this could be used as an example of how the Zerk semillon might look with that extra year's bottle age—it's lost a little of the fresh, lemony fruit that it had in its youth (although it's still nice and tangy) and is beginning to show hints of more mature, concentrated toast, honey and cream flavours. Very good value.
Available through Liquorland and Vintage Cellars.

1998 Leo Buring Clare Valley Semillon
☆ $12.00

While the Leo Buring name was built on great, long-lived rieslings and dark, rich multi-district red blends, some excellent well-priced wines made from other white grape varieties have appeared over the last few years. This is one example—a sensationally zesty, bold white wine with round, lemony fruit and lots of that alluring, complex, highly enjoyable toasty flavour semillon seems to develop after a year or so in the bottle. Along with the Barossa, the Clare is South Australia's other best semillon-producing region and this is a good example of the style.

1998 Moculta Barossa Semillon $13.95

Even though the Hunter Valley is considered Australia's best semillon region, the Barossa Valley in South Australia dominates this list of recommendations. You can see why in wines like the Moculta from Barossa Valley Estates—it's been aged carefully in wood and has a full, soft, almost creamy texture to enhance the round, lemony, fresh grape-pulpy flavours you get in the region's semillon. Great wine for easy summer's quaffing.

2000 Morris Rutherglen Semillon $12.95

Rutherglen and Morris are two names you would hardly expect to see associated with semillon (you'd be more comfortable to find them on a bottle of luscious muscat or heroic, beefy red), but this warm, inland region in north-east Victoria is obviously capable of producing lovely, dry white wine from the grape. In fact, Max picked this in the blind tasting as a 'classic' example of Hunter Valley semillon, with its very pale colour, its lightness, its green pea-like aromas and its very dry, crisp, lanolin-like flavours. Drink young and fresh over the summer.

1996 Mount Pleasant Elizabeth Hunter Valley Semillon $14.95

What book about Australia's best cheap wines could be complete without this? Lizzie is a true classic—produced in the traditional Hunter style (low alcohol, unwooded, very lean) and aged for four years in the bottle before release, even at close to our $15 cut-off mark it's still great value: rich, toasty, pineappley smells make you think it's going to be full-bodied and oaky, but when you get it in the mouth it's lean, crisp, juicy and light. Simply a benchmark wine.

2000 Peter Lehmann Barossa Valley Semillon
M ⭐ $12.00

One of the best value semillons we tasted. Bursting at the seams with fresh, sweet lemon-juicy smells and flavours, this lightly wooded, tangy, crisp white wine is exceptionally well-made, with just enough careful oak maturation to fill out the texture in the mouth, and just enough fruit sweetness to keep you coming back for more. Drink while young and bouncy, or keep for a few years to mellow and develop.

2000 Richmond Grove Hunter Valley Semillon
$14.95

Part of the ever-expanding range of Richmond Grove regional varietal wines (you'll come across others throughout the book), this is a great example of a traditional light, lean unwooded Hunter semillon which, while worth keeping to develop complexity, is almost too lovely to resist right now. Almost sauvignon blanc-like in its grassy, aromatic green pea characters, it's so crisp, fresh and zingy that you're almost overcome by the urge to find a big plate of prawns and take the rest of the afternoon off.

2000 Rosemount Estate Diamond Label Semillon
$14.95

A few years ago, Rosemount departed from their usual oak-matured semillon style and released an unwooded, traditional Hunter style. It wasn't, unfortunately, well received (except by Hunter-loving wine writers like us), so the style has changed back. It's by no means oaky, though: in fact at this young stage, it's all about excellent fresh, fragrant green pea and grassy intensity, with a very crisp, very dry and zesty palate.

1999 Tyrrell's HVD Hunter Valley Semillon
P $14.95

This is classic youthful Hunter Valley semillon from a classic site—the Hunter Valley Distillery vineyard planted in 1908. And it's a steal at the price. Why? Because it has all the hallmarks of being able to develop in the bottle for five, 10, even 20 years to become an incredibly complex dry white wine (if it's cellared properly). It's very pale, almost colourless, almost neutral in flavour, but with this intense, very dry, chalky, lemony tightness. Indeed, unless you're used to the style, you may not enjoy it all that much at this young age—although it would be pretty lip-smackingly good with seafood.
Available through Cellarmasters:
call 1800 500 260 or visit
www.cellarmasters.com.au

2000 Yalumba Barossa Semillon
$14.95

A style stablemate of the Peter Lehmann semillon, this is young Barossa white wine at its most endearingly boisterous. Surprisingly aromatic and sweet-smelling, with hints of green apple and fresh-cut grass, it has the most wonderful crisp, refreshing, intense, lingering juiciness. Again, you could buy a few and age them for a couple of years, but why bother when it's so delicious right now?

OTHER WHITE VARIETALS

This section deals with the range of non-classic grape varieties planted in Australia. Particularly prominent are the Portuguese variety verdelho, and chenin blanc, a native of the Loire, both of which are at their best in the warmish climates of the Swan Valley, the Hunter, Langhorne Creek and McLaren Vale. Most of these wines are unwooded and are largely enjoyable for their freshness and abundant ripe, fruity flavours.

 Quaff! Award Winner   ★ Best Buy   M Max's Pick   P Peter's Pick

**2000 Bleasdale
Verdelho
M $13.95**

A terrific vintage for this Langhorne Creek producer. The unwooded Bleasdale Verdelho, from the Sandhill vineyard, has rarely looked better than this: it has wonderful, tropical fruit perfumes, delicious tangy, ripe, sweet passionfruit characters and a crisp, clean finish that lingers. The 2000 Verdelho is fresh, full, vibrant, flavoursome and close to irrestible.

**2000 Brown Bros
Chenin Blanc
$12.50**

With each wine that they release Brown Brothers have a clear idea of their target market. This youngster will appeal to those who enjoy whites that are fresh, fruity and sweet. The grapes were picked at different levels of ripeness over the period of a month to provide additional interest on the palate: the wine has tropical fruit, lemon and apple flavours and a finish that is clean and sweet.

**2000 Charles Sturt
Pinot Gris
$14.95**

The Charles Sturt University at Wagga Wagga is one of our key centres for training winemakers and viticulturists. The attached winery serves the dual function of making commercial wines and training emerging winemakers. The 2000 Pinot Gris is showing its youth at the moment but has some varietal spiciness with slightly flowery, melon and hay flavours, mid-palate softness and a crisp, dry finish.

**2000 Coriole
Chenin Blanc
$13.95**

This medium-sized McLaren Vale producer is well-regarded for the quality of its unwooded chenin and the 2000 harvest has produced a wine that is every bit as good as its best. It has perfumed, grassy characters on the nose and a palate that features sweet tropical fruit with some grassiness. This clean, fresh lively white has lovely lingering flavours and a crisp, zingy, dry finish.

2000 Dowie Doole Chenin Blanc $12.50

The fourth vintage of this wine has been sourced from 42-year-old vines at the Tintookie vineyard at Blewitt Springs in McLaren Vale. The property is owned by Dowie Doole partners Drew Dowie and Lulu Lunn and the viticulture is in Lunn's obviously capable hands. While the owners lament that these old vines have once again produced a small crop, we are grinning because it means that the wine has a pleasing concentration of flavour. And the price means it's great value. Clear varietal chenin blanc characters are the highlight of this easy-drinking white: passionfruit, banana-lemon, tropical fruits with a hint of grassiness. It is lively, fresh, soft and round with delicious lingering flavours and crisp acidity.

1999 Half Mile Creek Verdelho $12.00

Half Mile Creek is the reincarnation of the old Augustine winery in Mudgee. This varietal, however, was made by Robert Guadagnini from Hunter Valley fruit which was transported after night harvesting to Mudgee. It is a cracker: fresh, clean and lively with vibrant, ripe tropical fruit flavours. A soft, easy-quaffing, unwooded white that represents great value.

1999 Hamilton Chenin Blanc $13.95

This is an excellent example of oak-matured chenin produced from McLaren Vale fruit and matured in French oak casks. It has leesy, barrel fermentation aromas and toasty oak, butterscotch and hazelnut flavours and is fresh, lively and pristine with good fruit intensity to balance its classy oak.

2000 Lamont's Verdelho P $14.95

This resurgent producer is a necessary stop for any wine lover visiting the Swan Valley. Its restaurant and outdoor eating areas serve the region's best food and it has a thoughtfully equipped art gallery and tastefully designed cellar door area. Best of all, the wines under Mark Warren's direction are outstanding. Fruit for these come from the Lamont estate vineyard. The wine is pressed gently and only the first, free-run juices are used to emphasise delicacy and retain purity of fruit flavour. The 2000 Lamont's Verdelho is intensely perfumed with luscious tropical fruit, is soft, round and full flavoured, with ripe passionfruit, nectarine and sweet tropical fruit characters and has a crisp, dry finish that lingers.

1998 Mallee Point Cavardella ☆ $9.95

Mallee Point is yet another label from the adventurous John Casella of Griffith and the grape variety is one that he believes is unique to the Casella winery. During the 1960s, Filippa and Maria Casella bought a property in the Riverina on which they found 20 vines. They named it Cavardella as a play on the name of another of their properties, Cavergrande, in the foothills of Mt Etna in Sicily and their family name, Casella. They used the original vines to plant about a hectare on their house block which is the source of this wine. They had the cavardella DNA tested in 1999 and it didn't match any known varieties. Both the story and the wine have been a terrific surprise to us both. The Mallee Point Cavardella is remarkably fresh for a wine that is almost three years old. As Max says 'not dissimilar to a young Hunter semillon with tangy lanolin and lemongrass flavours and a lean, refreshing palate.' Peter loved its 'spicy, savoury flavours and its minerally, pebbly qualities'.

1999 Mitchelton
Viognier
$14.95

One of the most ethereal and exotic tasting of all grape varieties, viognier (pronounced vee-on-yay) is a native of the Rhône Valley where it is best known as the extraordinarily expensive wine from Condrieu. Viognier has become increasingly popular in Australia thanks to the pioneering work of Yalumba. One of the keys to its success is ensuring that the vines are low yielding, otherwise the wine will be dilute and bland. Don Lewis and his team at Mitchelton have worked hard to keep yields low by not using irrigation and by pruning the vines to thirty fruitful buds. The wine is tank fermented with the temperature held at 10°C in order to retain varietal perfumes. With all this effort, we would have expected a more expensive wine—once again, the quaffer benefits. Max enjoyed the Mitchelton's 'terrific lime blossom and excellent aromatic, fragrant qualities' while Peter was attracted by 'its viscous texture, dried apricot and honeysuckle flavours'. Don't expect bold overt characters: this is a subtle white with delicacy and finesse. **Available at cellar door only. Call (03) 5736 2221.**

1999 Moondah Brook Verdelho $12.95

While this is not a great example of the Moondah Brook Verdelho, it's a pretty pleasant white: clean, fresh with some sweet tropical fruit flavours and a lively dryish finish. The 2000 should be even better.

2000 Paul Conti 'The Tuarts' Chenin Blanc $14.95

Although not so well known outside Western Australia, this small family winery has been established at Wanneroo for more than half a century. Paul Conti and his son Jason have three vineyards in this part of the Swan District including the Tuarts vineyard at Carabooda (established in 1980) from which the fruit for this wine has been sourced. Another good example of chenin, it has lovely, fat, grassy, tropical and pineapple flavours which are balanced by crisp, lemony acidity.

1999 Seaview Verdelho $7.00

Seaview has largely focused on the production of wine from the McLaren Vale, but with this white it has extended its horizons to two other regions which are exemplary growers of verdelho; the Hunter

Valley and Langhorne Creek. This delicious wine has excellent ripe, sweet, tropical fruit, is plump and fleshy yet with some fineness and delicate balance and finishes clean, fresh and quite dry. At the price, it's a stunner. One of the great bargains.

2000 Swanbrook Chenin Blanc $14.80

Swanbrook is the phoenix-like revival of the former Swan Valley home of Evans and Tate, now owned by restaurateur John Andreou, who is more than ably assisted by winemaker Rob Marshall. They processed 500 tonnes in their first year and are selling almost half of this under the Swanbrook label. Some of the chenin was barrel fermented in new French barriques but the dominant character is the fruitiness of the chenin grape. It has delicate perfumes, fresh, clean tropical and guava flavours and overly crisp acidity on the finish. Expect that to soften with a few months in the bottle. Best with food. Limited availability all states except SA. Call (08) 9296 3100 or email swanbrookwines@optusnet.com.au

2000 Swanbrook Verdelho $14.80

The standout wine from Swanbrook has heaps of flavour: pungent grassy aromas, lemony herbal and passionfruit characters and a crisp, grassy edge. It is soft and fleshy with good weight and reasonable length. Impressive. Limited availability all states except SA. Call (08) 92963100 or email swanbrookwines@optusnet.com.au

1999 Tahbilk Marsanne
$12.99

You'll get the whole story of Tahbilk Marsanne on pages 99–100. In most years, the wine is quite aromatic with youthful, estery, honeysuckle characters. This vintage will serve as a good introduction to it, athough it is in a slightly different style: more lean and nutty with almondy flavours. As always, a good drop.

1999 Tulloch Verdelho
$14.00

The Tulloch winery is now part of the Southcorp group and specialises in the varietal table wines that the Hunter Valley does best. So it'll come as no surprise that theirs is typically one of the best produced in that region. It is an unoaked white made to emphasise its fruity characters while it's young and fresh. This is a full-flavoured example of the Hunter style: ripe nectarine and tropical fruit flavours, rich and viscous with some sweetness on the finish.

2000 Primo Estate 'La Biondina' Colombard
$14.95

The Primo Estate vineyard and winery is located in the hot, fertile country just to the north of Adelaide's metropolitan sprawl, and its brilliant young winemaker, Joe Grilli, regularly produces some of the most exciting wines we can think of. Here he has managed to turn a high-yielding, much-maligned grape variety, colombard, into one of Australia's most reliably refreshing unwooded white wines. Absolutely bursting with fresh passionfruit and rockmelon flavours, its lively touch of sweetness is superbly balanced by a zingy, more-ish dryness.

TAHBILK MARSANNE

Tahbilk is one of Australia's oldest and most picturesque wineries, situated on the banks of the Goulburn River about 120 kilometres north of Melbourne. Local Aborigines called the place 'tabilk-tabilk' meaning 'place of many waterholes'. The winery was established in 1860 and is currently run by fourth generation winemaker Alister Purbrick, whose family have owned the winery since 1925.

Tahbilk's best known wines are the 1860 Vines Shiraz and the Marsanne. The former is made from vines planted in the winery's first year of operation, which are among the oldest shiraz vines in the world. Marsanne was planted at Tahbilk in the late 1860s although, unlike the shiraz, those vines have not survived. The 40 hectares of marsanne currently in production have two claims to fame. Firstly, it is the largest single vineyard planting of this grape variety in the world. Secondly, it includes vines planted in 1927, thought to be the oldest marsanne in the world.

Marsanne is a native of the Rhône Valley (in the south of France) where it is most noteworthy in Hermitage and St Joseph. It is also found in Switzerland, California and Australia, where it has found a home-from-home in Victoria's Goulburn Valley. Here contrasting styles are produced by neighbours Tahbilk, which chooses to make an unwooded marsanne, and Mitchelton, whose marsanne is wood aged. Both wines have their supporters although Tahbilk get the popular vote as they produce a whopping 35 000 cases a year, much more than any other single producer in the world. They expect to increase this in the next few years to between 45 000 and 50 000 cases—with that volume to sell, you know they'll keep the price reasonable.

Tahbilk Marsanne has long enjoyed a reputation as one of Australia's best value-for-money wines. You can drink it while it is young for its fresh, clean, fruity flavours or cellar it for five to seven years or more and savour its mellow, toasty, honeyed characters and gentle acidity.

Max recently tasted seven vintages of the Tahbilk Marsanne from the current release back to 1985 to get some indication of the way the wine matures with age. The 1998 had floral, honeysuckle and tropical fruit flavours and was crisp and dry on the finish while the 1996 had already developed some toastiness but remained fresh and lively with a gentle, creamy finish. The 1994 vintage showed less development, and therefore less toasty character, but was gentler, softer and rounder than the younger wines. The 1992 was fully mature, mellow, rich, honeyed with lively yet gentle acidity. Although the wines from 1990 and 1985 were past their best, the 1988 showed just how well these marsannes can age. It had rich, concentrated lemon citrus fruit with some toastiness, was rounded, mellow and complex, yet was lively and had crisp acidity on the finish: an outstanding wine drinking at its peak. (And well under $10 when it was released.)

Our preference is for the young, fresh Tahbilk Marsanne at between one and two years of age as it's a delightfully fruity summer drink at a very reasonable price. But we have enjoyed many mature examples of the style and, with rare exceptions, we have been very impressed. If you have good cellaring facilities, perhaps you should buy a dozen bottles, drink 10 in the first few years and keep two for between five and seven years.

SEMILLON SAUVIGNON BLANC BLENDS

Those few semillon sauvignon blancs recommended here represent a very impressive group of wines. Although more expensive than the semillon chardonnay or other white blends, they are of significantly greater quality, and therefore better value.

The secret is the lift, that tangy, zingy quality which sauvignon blanc provides when it comes from premium regions such as Margaret River, McLaren Vale, the Barossa and Great Southern. The Margaret River has made this blend its own with the success that it has enjoyed—its grassy, herbal semillon seems to marry with sauvignon blanc in a way that is not repeated anywhere else in the world. What we are delighted to see is several wines sourced from this region at everyday prices—the production of larger volumes of these wines, more sustainable yields and machine harvesting have all helped winemakers to keep prices down.

These are bistro whites, made to be drunk while they are young, fresh and flavoursome: quaffing whites to be gulped without much thought over a summer lunch at your favourite café. Unmistakably Australian.

 Quaff! Award Winner ★ Best Buy M Max's Pick P Peter's Pick

**2000 Cape Mentelle
Georgiana
P M $14.95**

An absolutely seductive blend of sauvignon blanc and semillon with a dash of chenin blanc, sourced from the Cape Mentelle estate and other Margaret River growers. Unlike this winery's benchmark semillon sauvignon blanc, this is an unwooded blend picked early in the season. The emphasis here is on freshness, vibrance and ripe varietal fruit characters. This is only the second vintage which has been widely available. The stunning 1999 harvest has been followed by one described by the normally taciturn David Hohnen (General Manager of Cape Mentelle) as 'near perfect' and the wine shows it. Peter loved its zingy, passionfruit flavours and lively crisp acidity while Max just grinned and nodded. Think summer!

**2000 Coriole Semillon
Sauvignon Blanc
$14.95**

This medium-sized McLaren Vale producer has long enjoyed a reputation for the quality of its semillon. Add to that the region's affinity with reasonably priced sauvignon blanc and you'll not be surprised to learn that this unoaked blend is a winner. It has fabulous, tropical fruit perfumes, fresh, clean passionfruit, green bean and grassy flavours and a soft, gentle finish. This is a pristine white with round, fleshy texture, ripe sweet fruit and cleansing acidity. Coriole's favourite wine and food match is their Semillon Sauvignon Blanc with a slice of very good bread covered with Paula Jenkin's Woodside Goat Curd drizzled with extra virgin olive oil and crushed black pepper. It's not every winery that owns a cheese company and produces olive oil!

1999 Crofters Semillon Sauvignon Blanc $14.95

The excellent value-for-money Crofters label is named after the historic homestead (built *circa* 1863) which is currently the BRL Hardy state headquarters at the picturesque Houghton property in the Swan Valley. Chief winemaker, Larry Cherubino, has fashioned a lively white from grapes brought in from around Western Australia, including Frankland and Margaret River. It has some herbal aromatics, is clean and lively with good depth of greengage and green bean flavours and a crisp, dry finish.

2000 Evans and Tate Margaret River Classic $14.95

Which came first, the café society or this popular icon of that group of trend setters? Whatever the answer, this flavoursome, easy-drinking white has been one of the West's most popular wines for over a decade. Now it's back where it started, as a Margaret River wine and with a more modest price tag. The higher yields that Evans and Tate can get from their Jindong vineyard in the warmer north-east of Margaret River result in savings which are passed on to the consumer. Now the Classic is a blend of semillon, sauvignon blanc, verdelho and chardonnay sourced from both Jindong and Willyabrup further to the south. It has a pungent grassiness, tropical fruit and grassy flavours, is clean, fresh and lively and has zesty acidity on the finish.

1999 Goundrey Classic White $14.95

Rapid expansion has been the order of the day since Jack Bendat took over this Mount Barker winery: production is now over 200 000 cases per year. Their vibrant semillon sauvignon blanc blend represents good value: it has ripe, passionfruit perfumes, a round, pulpy texture, a neat balance between tropical fruit and herbaceous, grassy flavours and some crisp, cleansing, green acidity.

1999 Grant Burge Virtuoso $14.80

Grant Burge is a larger-than-life promoter of the Barossa Valley and this blend of sauvignon blanc and semillon (roughly 50–50) comes from different parts of the region which he calls home. It's a wine that we like, in the sweeter, riper, more tropical style. There are attractive gooseberry and other tropical perfumes and lychees, gooseberry and sweet tropical fruit characters with some underlying grassiness. This fresh and lively quaffer is soft, full-flavoured and easy to drink.

1999 Orlando Trilogy Semillon Sauvignon Blanc Muscadelle ☆ $13.95

As the popular Orlando sparkling wine Trilogy paid homage to the three grape varieties of Champagne (chardonnay, pinot noir and pinot meunier), so Orlando is marketing this as a tribute to the dry white blends of Bordeaux (semillon, sauvignon blanc and muscadelle—generally known as tokay in Australia). The semillon and sauvignon blanc comes from the Barossa and McLaren Vale while the muscadelle is sourced from the cooler Eden Valley. Not surprisingly, the taste is Australia not France. It has herbal aromas, a clean, fresh lively palate with some zing, a pulpy texture, ripe gooseberry flavour and an intense, crisp finish.

2000 Rosemount Semillon Sauvignon Blanc $11.95

This is a remarkably good wine at the price thanks, in particular, to an outstanding vintage for semillon in the Hunter Valley. Chief wine-maker Philip Shaw is very clever at sourcing wines throughout Australia and, in this case, he has pulled in the sauvignon blanc from the Hunter, Margaret River, the Strathbogies and McLaren Vale. The 2000 Semillon Sauvignon Blanc has pronounced green pea aromas, some herbal and tropical fruit characters and lively cleansing acidity. This is a light yet intense, zesty white that has good crispness and impressive concentration of flavour.

1999 Xanadu Semillon Sauvignon Blanc $14.00

In the past few years, there has been dramatic expansion at this long established Margaret River winery following changes in ownership. Consumers are the big winners as Xanadu now has four wines available in the under $15 price bracket. This is a Margaret River blend of 65 per cent semillon and 35 per cent sauvignon blanc, but with a difference. Unlike the other wines reviewed here, a large proportion of the semillon has been barrel fermented in new French puncheons giving it some toasty characters on the nose and some creaminess on the palate. The excellent 1999 harvest has produced a clean, fresh dry white that has grassy, herbal flavours and a crisp, lively finish.

SEMILLON CHARDONNAY BLENDS

This is a particularly Australian style. Almost no other country in the world blends these two grape varieties—indeed, we can't help noticing that Californian winemakers are beginning to cash in on the style. It is popular with Australian wineries sourcing fruit from the irrigated areas along the Murray.

In most instances, price has been the key selling point—and this is the case again in the wines we recommend. However, unless it is made with the care, attention to detail and relatively low yields of a wine like the Jacob's Creek—which could rightly be regarded as the epitome of the style—this blend can appear dilute, bland and lacking in flavour. Some fruit from cooler regions can provide a lift and that has happened with wines like the Poet's Corner, the Rosemount and the Xanadu. From 29 wines tasted, we have recommended the best six examples of the blend.

 Quaff! Award Winner   ★ Best Buy   Max's Pick   Peter's Pick

1999 Bethany 'The Manse' Semillon Riesling Chardonnay ☆ $9.00

The Schrapel family have been growing grapes in the Barossa Valley for more than 150 years and Geoff and Rob Schrapel are fifth generation custodians of the land. This wine comes from their Barossa holdings and is a blend of semillon (50 per cent), riesling (30 per cent) and chardonnay (20 per cent). It is a decent, straightforward quaffer with some toasty characters, a pleasant mouthfeel enhanced by a touch of sweetness and gentle acidity. Great price.

1999 Brook Ridge Semillon Chardonnay ☆ $5.99

This is the ultra cheapie from Liquorland which we preferred to the $7 Vintage Cellars Quaffing White and to the Brook Ridge Shiraz Cabernet. It is simple, light-bodied and very good for the price: a clean, refreshing drink with a murmur of semillon grassiness and a whisper of slightly fatter chardonnay.
Available through Liquorland and Vintage Cellars.

2000 Jacob's Creek Semillon Chardonnay Ⓜ ☆ $8.95

Another reliable budget-priced white from Chief Winemaker Phil Laffer and the folks at Orlando. It emphasises how well the irrigated vineyards along the Murray can produce consistent quality wines of some character. This stylish wine is clean, fresh, soft and round and very easy to drink, has some light grassy perfumes and flavours that range from ripe tropical fruits to zesty, grassy characters.

2000 Poet's Corner Semillon Sauvignon Blanc Chardonnay

❶! P ☆$ $9.95

Mudgee is becoming fashionable—hard to believe, but true—and it's wines like this that are responsible. Poet's Corner is the second label for the Mudgee-based Montrose which is part of the expansive Orlando Wyndham group. The label celebrates a local boy who became one of Australia's greatest poets—writer of bush ballads and short stories, Henry Lawson. The 2000 Poet's Corner white blend shows pungent herbal aromas and full-bodied green pea and herbal flavours, is clean, fresh, lively and powerful with a crisp, zesty finish. Great value.

2000 Rosemount Semillon Chardonnay

$11.95

This is another example of Rosemount stretching its boundaries across the country to find the ingredients for this easy-drinking white blend. The semillon comes from their home vineyards in the Hunter as well as the plains of the Murray Valley while the chardonnay is sourced from McLaren Vale (which is looking more and more a Rosemount stronghold), as well as the Hunter and Murray valleys. The 2000 harvest was ideal in the Hunter but much more difficult in the South Australian regions. Chief Winemaker Philip Shaw has opted for a touch more complexity by giving some of the chardonnay a couple of months in oak. The 2000 Rosemount Semillon Chardonnay is a straightforward, easy-drinking white with a pleasant mouthfeel, some apple and tropical fruit flavours and a hint of sweetness on the finish.

1999 Xanadu Secession and 2000 Xanadu Secession $14.00

Nothing suggests that Xanadu is heading in the right direction more clearly than the latest vintage of their mainstream white blend. We are happy to recommend the 1999 Secession—a blend of semillon and chardonnay. It has grassy, grapefruit skin, herbal flavours, a creamy texture and is cool, clean and crisp.

But this new harvest has produced a much better wine, which we tasted as this book was just about to go to print. The 2000 Xanadu Secession is a blend of semillon (46 per cent), sauvignon blanc (27 per cent), chenin blanc (17 per cent) and chardonnay (10 per cent), was sourced from Margaret River and Frankland and represents the style Xanadu wish to pursue in the future. It has voluminous passionfruit and gooseberry aromas, is fresh, lively, soft and round with attractive sweet fruit: passionfruit, lychees and some herbal notes. This is a tangy, vibrant, full-flavoured white with crisp, zingy acidity. Delicious.

OTHER WHITE BLENDS

It's a bit of an undistinguished title, really, isn't it: other white blends; it doesn't do justice to the often sunshine-ripe, enticing, highly quaffable flavours you'll find in many of the dry white wines in this chapter. But it was the only way we could think to group together those whites that are neither varietal (chardonnay, for example, or riesling) nor a 'traditional' blend (semillon and sauvignon blanc, for example). So this is where you'll find non-traditional blends of chardonnay and sauvignon, and generic blends like the classic quaffer, Houghton White Burgundy (it seems fitting that Houghton's home state, Western Australia, has provided over half the recommended wines).

However, it's worth noting that while we are recommending a fairly healthy nine wines here—with over half of them under $12—we also tasted many that were, to be frank, dilute, unbalanced, clumsily oaked and just plain boring. We wouldn't go so far as to suggest you avoid cheap generic white blends in favour of varietal wines (not when you can find wines like those listed here), but we do feel that too many winemakers are placing their cheap white blends very low down in the pecking order and aren't perhaps taking as much care with fruit sourcing and production as they are with the more prestigious premium wines.

Q! Quaff! Award Winner   **★** Best Buy   **M** Max's Pick   **P** Peter's Pick

1999 Alkoomi Mount Frankland White
P M $14.40

Alkoomi was one of the first and is now one of the best producers in the Frankland district of the remote Great Southern region of Western Australia. While many of Alkoomi's wines deserve their $20-plus price tag, we were delighted to find this delicious white for under $15. A blend of various white varieties, but it's the distinctive grassy, zesty flavours contributed by the semillon and sauvignon blanc that give the wine its incisive freshness and bone dry intensity.

1999 Elderton Tantalus
$13.95

Neither chenin blanc nor sauvignon blanc are particularly well regarded by Barossa winemakers—the former variety suffers from a terrible image problem, the latter is a variety that many would argue needs a much cooler climate to perform at its best. But this full-flavoured white from Elderton has managed to completely sidestep all the negativity and combine chenin blanc and sauvignon blanc (with a splash of chardonnay) in a tangy, oaky, white with bold pineapple and vanilla characters and broad appeal.

1999 Fox River Classic White
$14.95

Fox River is the second label of the large Goundrey winery at Mount Barker in Western Australia. We liked quite a few Fox River wines in our tastings and found them to exhibit good regional and varietal characters at an attractive price. This blend of chenin blanc and semillon tastes more like a 2000 vintage wine than a 1999, because it's just so youthful, zesty and fresh, with very aromatic green apple fruit flavours and a crisp, lively finish.

1999 Hardys Insignia Chardonnay Sauvignon Blanc $11.95

It's a good indication of the overall standard of winemaking at Hardys that so many of their cheaper wines are recommended in this book. This wine from the usually reliable Insignia range is a good example—a gold medal winner at a national wine show, it's a refreshing, clean, lemony blend of fruit-driven chardonnay and aromatic sauvignon blanc. The 1999 vintage, which may also be out there in bottleshop land, is a little fuller-flavoured, with a savoury, oaky background to the fruit flavours.

2000 Houghton White Burgundy ☆ $10.95

You'll find the full story on this classic quaffer on pages 114–117. It's enough to say here that the 2000 vintage of this, one of Australia's most popular white wines, is exactly as we expected it to be: extremely lively, fresh and fruity, with sunny yellow peach and melon flavours and a juicy round softness.

Non Vintage Moondah Maritime White $9.95

This is a non-vintage wine (a blend of wine from more than one year) which is unusual in a bottled table wine; you'd expect it in a cheap cask, but not necessarily in a wine that sells for almost ten bucks a pop. We liked the wine for its ripe, peachy, tropical pulpy roundness in the mouth—its sheer sunshine-packed flavour. A good, if slightly sweet (despite what the label says) example of how the chenin blanc grape (which dominates this blend) produces very friendly flavours in West Australian conditions.

2000 Rosemount Estate
New Australian White
⭐ $8.95

A blend of chardonnay, sauvignon blanc and verdelho, fermented in stainless steel and bottled (and hopefully sold and drunk) as young as possible—the idea is for Rosemount's new Australian range to generate an excitement about the new vintage wines coming on to the market soon after the grapes have been picked. Not complex or long-tasting, just crisp, clean, juicy, perfumed with ripe citrus fruit and highly drinkable— especially well-chilled on a hot day.

2000 Ryecroft Flame
Tree White
⭐ $7.95

This is a remarkably similar wine to the Rosemount New Australian White...it's also a blend of chardonnay, sauvignon blanc and verdelho fermented in stainless steel, and it's also clean, juicy, perfumed with ripe citrus fruit and highly drinkable. In fact, the only differences that we make out are the label and the price. Oh, and by the way, Ryecroft is owned by Rosemount Estate.

1999 St Hallett
Poachers Blend
$13.00

An unusual blend of chenin blanc, semillon, riesling and sauvignon blanc—but unusual only in that these four grapes rarely share the same bottle space, as the flavours are very familiar. This is the Barossa Valley at its everyday quaffing white wine best: full of ripe, creamy, tropical flavour, very fresh, soft and round in the mouth, altogether a remarkably easy drink. We also tasted the 2000 vintage of the Poachers Blend on a number of occasions and have to report that we weren't as impressed—it lacks the fruit intensity and life of the 1999.

classic quaffers

HOUGHTON WHITE BURGUNDY

Without question, it was the Houghton White Burgundy (HWB) that put the Western Australian wine industry on the map, and it did this before the popular areas of Margaret River and the Great Southern were planted with vineyards. Amazingly, for an Australian wine, it has been produced at each vintage for more than 60 years and for much of this time it has been one of Australia's best selling dry white wines. At present, more HWB than ever before is bottled—160 000 cases a year—making it second only to Queen Adelaide Chardonnay in the domestic sales stakes.

The HWB is affectionately regarded by its legion of followers throughout Australia and overseas as a flavoursome white that is sold at an affordable price. In the European Union, it has been known as Houghton Supreme and HWB because burgundy is a protected name. The Australian government has agreed to phase out the use of this term but has not set the date for this to happen. Houghton are keen to retain the name in Australia for as long as is legally possible.

The wine will be forever linked to the legendary Houghton winemaker, Jack Mann, who worked for the company for more than 50 vintages and pioneered the style. It is generally thought that the first Houghton White Burgundy came from the 1937 harvest. A similar wine, known as Houghton's Hock, had been made for several years during the 1930s. However, according to Jack Mann's daughter, Corin Lamont, the company did not make a successful dry white wine until after they purchased a Seitz filter in 1937. A chenin blanc made by Jack Mann from that vintage won the trophy for the best dry white table wine at the 1937 Melbourne Show. The decision was made to give it a name change and Houghton White Burgundy came into being. With the subsequent vintage, Mann followed up his success by winning the trophy for best young dry white at the 1938 Melbourne Show.

Jack Mann believed that there were two things that set HWB apart from other wines of the time. Firstly, he did not pick the grapes for the wine until they were fully ripe. Secondly, the chenin blanc juice was kept in contact with its skins for 24 hours after the gentle initial crushing to encourage colour and to enhance flavour.

In its earliest years, Houghton White Burgundy was made from 100 per cent chenin blanc, although, at the time, the grape variety was thought to be semillon. The eminent American viticulturist Professor Harold Olmo, who was based at the University of Western Australia for eight months during 1955, working on the viticultural problems facing the wine industry in the Swan Valley, identified the grape variety as chenin blanc not semillon. Chenin blanc has remained the dominant grape variety. Muscadelle played a significant part in the blend and was an important component until the late 1980s, and both riesling and verdelho have been significant contributors at different times.

Since 1992, Houghton White Burgundy has been made from chenin blanc (50 per cent), chardonnay (20 per cent), semillon (15 per cent) and verdelho (5 per cent), with the remaining 10 per cent being riesling and muscadelle. It is predominantly sourced from the Swan Valley, though the proportion varies from 60–80 per cent depending on vintage. The balance comes from Frankland, Mount Barker, Pemberton, Margaret River and Moondah Brook. The chenin comes from the Swan and Moondah Brook. More chardonnay is about to come on stream and so it is expected that the proportion of this variety will be increased in the future.

In the last few years, the cropping levels of the chenin have been reduced, and winemaker Larry Cherubino believes that this has improved the texture of the wine by making it more fleshy. Remarkably, considering the price, there is some excellent quality fruit used in the blend, including one block of chenin on the Great Northern Highway near Houghton that has 100-year-old vines.

So although economics is important with a wine at this price, Houghton and its growers continually strive for greater complexity in the vineyard. The use of cooler climate fruit, from places like Pemberton, Frankland and Mount Barker, has contributed greater intensity to the blend.

While there will be variation in the wine from vintage to vintage, the HWB tends to show consistency from year to year. The flexibility that the company has with its choice of vineyards enables it to maintain quality, even in difficult harvests. That said, the HWB vineyards are carefully mapped and graded and growers are well looked after because of the importance of the wine in the company's portfolio.

The Houghton White Burgundy is a great each-way bet as it is fresh, clean and fruity when young, yet ages beautifully, so from about five to seven years of age it is transformed into toasty, honeyed nectar of rare quality. The Houghton Show Reserve is not a special blend, just the HWB released with several years bottle age. Naturally, this enhances its status as a bargain buy. The HWB regularly wins gold medals at Australian wine shows. Indeed the 1986 Houghton Show Reserve White Burgundy won three trophies at the 1992 Adelaide Show where the judges thought it was an exceptional aged Hunter semillon.

A recent tasting of the HWB at the winery confirmed our thoughts about the wine and was in line with similar tastings we've done in the past. The 1999 was fresh, fruity and lively, neatly balanced, quite tightly structured and with good weight and a cleansing dry finish. The 1998 was more perfumed, with more overt sweet fruit and tropical flavours, while the 1997 was leaner, more earthy and minerally with a hint of green pea and some delightful fleshiness. The warm vintage is evident in the 1996, which appears to be at the in-between stage, a bit lean and tight and needing time to look its best.

The first hint of toastiness, a honeyed character and some bottle aged complexity comes with the 1995 HWB, which is still fresh and lively on the palate with a crisp, dry finish. The 1994 is less toasty, more fruity although with some honeyed notes: it just needs time to develop further. Although the 1993 doesn't show any toasty character, it has a deep, golden colour and some nicely developed honeycomb and lime juice characters, still fresh, lively and fine with great weight and richness: a terrific wine. The 1992 has the best show results of all the HWBs—it has the deepest, golden colour and honeyed, limey flavours, is still tight, lively and fleshy and is superb drinking.

At its current price, you could buy a dozen bottles, drink nine or 10 in the next year or so and keep the remaining two or three for five to seven years—you'd enjoy a rare wine experience for a modest outlay.

RED
WINES

CASK REDS

According to the statistics, only about 10 per cent of the cask market is red wine. Ten per cent: doesn't sound like much; not worth bothering about, really. Winemakers (and wine drinkers) obviously prefer their cheap quaffing red in bottles these days. This is a good thing for bottled red wine at the very cheapest end of the market: the better grapes used previously to help lift the quality of casks are now being redirected into the bottle.

But this is a bad thing for the few red casks that have been left behind, if our tasting was anything to go by—the 35 or so we tried for this book yielded a disappointing number of recommendable wines. Too many were thin, sweet, unappealing and, in some cases, undrinkable. We also tried many stale, oxidised and out of condition examples—reflecting the higher demand for and higher turnover of cask whites. Too many producers had tried to mask the shortage of fruit flavour and quality by adding tannin (for structure), oak chips (for flavour) or even leaving some residual sugar (for sweetness and softness)—all techniques that result in unbalanced wines if not done very well. As our recommended wines show, there's no substitute for using better grapes.

Again, there is a surprising reluctance by wine producers to relinquish the outdated European terminology. While not, perhaps, as misleading for red casks as for white (who really cares any more that burgundy should indicate a wine with a softer finish than claret, as it did traditionally in Australian wine shows?), it would be heartening to see some more imagination among the big company marketing departments. The old names will have to go one day—why not start replacing them sooner rather than later?

There is, after all, a predicted oversupply of red grapes just around the corner, and red casks could well be drummed into service to cope with it all. The clever producers are taking steps to anticipate this—one is even contemplating introducing a new 'pressings style' cask, in recognition of Morris' success with its (non-European) brand name. It's worth acknowledging that four of the five wines we recommend—Banrock, Renmano and both Hardys wines—are made by BRL Hardy. This says a lot for this company's positive attitude towards the red cask market.

As we did after tasting our way through the white casks, we've arrived at some general tips for buying red casks:

- again, smaller casks tend to contain better quality wine and represent better value (with the exception, perhaps, of the Morris Pressings, which comes in a whopping 10 litre box if you should so desire);
- casks labelled varietally (merlot, shiraz, etc) or even as blends of varieties (shiraz cabernet, for example) tend to be better than those with generic labels such as 'classic dry red' or with protected European names such as claret or burgundy.

All casks are 4 litres unless otherwise specified. And while some are actually more than $15, their equivalent 750ml bottle price is much lower than $15, so we felt they were worthy of inclusion.

Q! Quaff! Award Winner   Best Buy   **M** Max's Pick   **P** Peter's Pick

Banrock Station Shiraz Cabernet (2 litre)
P $12.95

This is a lighter bodied, really quite bold, fresh red wine with some spicy, grapey, cherry characters. Highly gluggable stuff.

Hardys Shiraz (3 litre)
$16.95

It's not easy to get good varietal fruit flavour into wine at this price, but this has it: dark, brambly berry shiraz flavours with ripe, medium-bodied plummy texture and a savoury lick of oak. Good cask red.

Hardys Merlot (3 litre)
$16.95

It's even harder to get good varietal flavour from the merlot grape at this price, but again, this tastes like it's meant to: attractive soft red fruits with a touch of herbal characters, smooth, light, easy and attractive.

Morris Pressings Style Dry Red
M $14.95

One for those who want their cask red big and butch. This has a reassuringly dark colour, winey, plummy, ripe, black fruit flavours and a fairly gutsy tannic grip. Heroic, quite rustic, red steak wine.

Renmano Shiraz Cabernet (2 litre)
$9.95

This good value quaffing red has round, dark purple fruit, some vanillin oak flavours softening the middle, and a fairly firm, plump finish.

SHIRAZ

Shiraz is unquestionably the greatest Aussie red wine variety and is popular at home and abroad. It certainly came up trumps in our tastings and proved conclusively that it offers something for everyone, at all price points. The most popular reds that we came across were from the Barossa Valley and McLaren Vale with Padthaway and Langhorne Creek also making, or contributing, to some marvellous wines available for under $15. However, there are delightfully different wines from regions such as the Hunter Valley, Great Southern and Goulburn Valley which you might not expect to squeeze into a book like this.

As might be expected, the shiraz available for under $10 tends to be sourced from close to the banks of the Murray. We've found some delightful, easy-drinking quaffers that we can recommend with confidence. Price has provided us with many of our worst nightmares as we have worked hard to keep the selection honest—and under $15. We have reluctantly left out some excellent wines such as the 1998 Normans Old Vines Shiraz and the 1998 Thomas & Thomas Langhorne Creek Shiraz, which we tasted believing they fitted our price point. Careful research suggested that these would not be widely available for under $15.

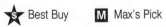 **Q!** Quaff! Award Winner   ★ Best Buy   **M** Max's Pick   **P** Peter's Pick

1998 Andrew Garrett Bold Shiraz
$14.95

There's no use pretending that you didn't know what you were buying: this brute of a wine is bold by name and certainly bold by nature—'Morris Pressings on steroids,' said Max in a quiet moment. Both of us felt that there are occasions when we would love to drink this hearty red: especially with a huge, juicy T-bone steak, fried onions and perfect chips. The fruit comes from the excellent 1998 harvest in Padthaway and McLaren Vale and the wine spent up to 15 months in American and French hogsheads, some of which were new. The Bold Shiraz has dark plum, aniseed and cedary oak flavours with some earthy, savoury characters, a silky smooth texture and chewy tannins on the finish.

1999 Barak's Bridge Shiraz
$14.95

Personal preference plays a big part in wine tasting and drinking, and Barak's Bridge is a case in point. Both of us have tried this wine a number of times: Peter loves its perfumed spicy aromas, supple, fleshy texture and firmish, lingering finish; while Max sees it hanging on the edge with juicy, green pepper characters. We expect some people to love this style and others to find it a tad unripe. Barak's Bridge is the second label of the Yarra Valley's Yering Station and is made from a blend of Yarra and Cowra grapes, which have been barrel fermented in French oak.

1998 Barossa Valley Estate Moculta Shiraz
M $13.95

Winemaker Natasha Mooney has fashioned a glorious, rich Barossa shiraz from the outstanding 1998 vintage. Barossa Valley

Estate, a large co-operative of growers in which BRL Hardy have taken a 50 per cent stake, has developed an enviable reputation for the quality of their reds over the past decade. While their E & E 'Black Pepper' Shiraz has attracted far too much attention from the overseas wine media (so reducing its availability in Australia), it has been their value-for-money labels such as Moculta that give us the greatest delight. This is a ripe, full-bodied, fleshy traditional Barossa shiraz, that has power, weight and generosity. Lashings of sweet black cherry and blackberry fruit and vanillin oak flavours, silky smooth texture and fine ripe tannins. Stunning value.

2000 Cottlers Bridge Shiraz
⭐ **$8.75**

This is another label of the Riverina's Casella Wines. It is an easy-drinking, light-bodied red with subdued aromas, redcurrant and red cherry flavours, fleshy texture and a soft, fine finish.

1999 David Wynn Shiraz
$14.50

Both of us fell in love with this wine on a week's trip to Malaysia with Adam Wynn, where we became convinced it was the perfect partner for the pungent, exotic fruit durian. While it's unlikely that you will have the opportunity to try that combination (we don't expect to have the chance again), this unwooded red does go very well with a wide range of dishes. David Wynn is the second label for Mountadam and is sourced entirely from the Eden Valley where the winery is situated. It is named after Adam's father, a pioneer of the Coonawarra, founder of Wynns, and the person credited with introducing the wine cask to Australian drinkers. Unwooded is the key: if you don't enjoy oaky reds, this might be what you are looking for. The 1999 David Wynn has attractive, spicy perfumes, lively peppery and redcurrant flavours, is soft, round and fleshy, and neatly balanced with a supple, gentle finish. Subtle, easy drinking.

2000 Deakin Estate
Shiraz
⭐ **$9.99**

In spite of the addition of 10 per cent ruby cabernet, this wine can legally be labelled as a shiraz. Sourced from along the Murray River, this is a terrific, youthful, easy-drinking red. It is well made with just a touch of oak, vibrant, ripe, raspberry, plum and macerated cherry flavours, fleshy texture and a soft, gentle finish. Uncomplicated.

1999 Deakin Select
Shiraz
$13.00

Previous vintages of this top wine from Deakin were released under the 'Alfred' label. It is 100 per cent shiraz made from grapes taken from four different sections of the Deakin home vineyard at Red Cliffs. In comparison with the standard Deakin Estate Shiraz, this is a bigger, medium- to full-bodied shiraz which has been pumped up by sweet, soft, coconutty oak—the result of 12 months maturation in mainly American oak, 85 per cent of which were new. It is fresh and lively with ripe black fruit, a silky texture and firm though not aggressive tannins. It has more power, richness and concentration of flavour than the standard shiraz and is worth putting aside for special occasions, or cellaring for six months to two years.

1999 Four Sisters Shiraz
$13.95

Mt Langi Ghiran produces one of this country's very best shiraz so Trevor Mast knows a thing or two about handling the variety. His second label pays tribute to his four daughters. Daliah, the oldest of them, has returned the compliment with her eye-catching, stylised label design. The Four Sisters Shiraz has dusty, spicy aromas, briary, peppery and black fruit flavours, is soft, round and lively with firm, fine tannins on the finish.

1999 Fox River Shiraz
$14.95

Fox River is the second label of the Mount Barker producer, Goundrey. The wine comes from vineyards in the Great Southern and spends 15 months in predominantly American oak before bottling. The 1999 Shiraz is a very good wine: spicy, ever so slightly stalky with white pepper edges and dark plum flavours. It has medium weight, is clean and well made with good concentration and reasonable power.

1998 Hardys Nottage Shiraz
$8.95

Nottage Hill has become one of BRL Hardys fighting brands and so the company works hard to maintain the quality/price ratio, to its customers' advantage. This is a multi-regional varietal sourced from South Australia's Riverland, Padthaway and Wrattonbully. Max believes this to be the most elegant of the three Nottage Hill reds while Peter admired its ripe perfumed fruit and juicy, spicy flavours. It has some raspberry and red plum characters, smooth texture and quite a firm finish. Better with dishes like spaghetti bolognese rather than quaffed by itself.

1998 Hardys Tintara Cellars Shiraz
$14.50

What a blockbuster this shiraz is! It is a product of grapes from McLaren Vale, Padthaway and the Adelaide Hills and has been given similar treatment to the Tintara Cellars Cabernet. This includes basket pressing, some open fermentation and some barrel fermentation in French and American oak (30 per cent of which was new) and 18 months barrel maturation. It is a dense, deep red with blackcurrant and spicy oak flavours that are well integrated. This is a full-bodied shiraz that has impressive power and weight and the ability to improve further with more bottle age.

1999 Haselgrove Sovereign Shiraz
$9.95

The benefits of being part of the rapidly expanding Cranswick empire must be readily apparent to this McLaren Vale producer, especially since the opening of its new 3000-tonne winery last February. Winemaking continuity is ensured with Nick Haselgrove still in charge, so it is no surprise to us that each wine in the Sovereign Series has made the grade for *Quaff!* The 1999 Shiraz is an attractive, light-weight, easy-drinking red with ripe raspberry, redcurrant and licorice flavours, and a clean, firm finish. Equally at home with the Sunday roast or your favourite mid-week sausage dish.

1999 Highwood Shiraz
McLaren Vale
$12.30

Here is another good wine from the McLaren Vale's Beresford Wines. It is fresh, soft, round and straightforward with ripe, spice, plum and blackcurrant flavours with a hint of oak in the background.

1999 Lindemans
Limestone Coast Shiraz
⭐ $10.15

The ability of Australia's largest companies to produce excellent quality wines at this price point never ceases to amaze us. Lindemans have had a long association with Coonawarra and most of the grapes for this wine are grown at nearby Padthaway and Robe, in the part of South Australia now known as the Limestone Coast. It's proving to be an excellent viticultural area with a cool, maritime climate, fertile soil and a good supply of underground water. The second vintage of the Limestone Coast Shiraz has light perfumes, bright, clean, sour cherry characters, a soft, smooth texture and a pleasant finish. This is a terrific wine for the price—flavoursome, uncomplicated and easy drinking.

**2000 McGuigan Bin
2000 Shiraz
$11.99**

A delightful, straightforward, easy-drinking red that is clean, fresh and vibrant with ripe plum and macerated cherry flavours and a soft, easy finish.

**1998 McGuigan
Shareholders Shiraz
$14.95**

A more full-bodied, powerful oaky shiraz that is supple and velvety with rich dark fruit flavours and substantial tannins. Its oakiness is balanced by the richness of the fruit.

**1998 McWilliams
Barossa Valley Shiraz
P $14.95**

This new regional range has made an impressive debut for McWilliams. This Barossa shiraz shows clear regional and varietal character, is reasonably priced, and is drinking beautifully. You want more? Well, it does come from an outstanding vintage. The wine is given a lift from being placed in new French and American oak for about eight days before being aged for 18 months in older American and French barrels. The American oak dominates, but with this wine that's no bad thing. Vanillin oak perfumes, ripe, squashy dark cherry, blackberry and briary oak flavours, a soft, creamy texture and fine, dry tannins. It's straightforward, glugable, a bit oaky and big and boisterous.

**1998 Mitchelton Shiraz
$14.95**

Winemaker Don Lewis consistently produces very good quality, reasonably priced shiraz. The 1998 is sourced from this Goulburn Valley producer's estate at Nagambie and from growers vineyards at Shepparton. The blend contains eight per cent mourvedre and a tiny amount of grenache and was aged for 18 months in two- and three-year-old French and American oak. The 1998 Mitchelton Shiraz has lifted, vanillin oak perfumes, is soft, round and fleshy with minty, red cherry flavours and a powerful tannic finish. It needs to be drunk alongside something like a hearty beef and red wine casserole and will benefit from cellaring for six months or so.

1996 Mount Pleasant Philip $14.95

An amazing wine for the price: a Hunter Valley shiraz released at four years of age and drinking at its peak. Mount Pleasant is the Hunter wing of McWilliams and specialises in local varietal wines. This might not appeal to everyone, as it's a distinctive traditional regional style: attractive charry oak aromas, supple, lively, dark cherry fruit made more complex by some earthy, leathery, tary characters. Soft, gentle, mellow and flavoursome.

1998 Orlando Jacob's Creek Reserve Shiraz $14.95

Seductive vanillin oak aromas; ripe blackcurrant, dark plum and chocolate flavours complexed by some spicy oak; silky texture; impressive weight, richness and power; quite a firm finish: the Jacob's Creek Reserve has it all. An impressive debut.

1999 Rosemount Shiraz $14.95

This Diamond Label Shiraz is one of Rosemount's great export successes. Fortunately, there's enough to go around the domestic market as well. Its popularity is hardly surprising when you consider that it is always consistent, flavour-packed, great value for money and oh-so-drinkable. It certainly shone in our tastings. The grapes come largely from Rosemount's extensive plantings in Langhorne Creek and the McLaren Vale, with a portion from Mudgee. There are some pleasing red berry aromas, the palate is soft, gentle and fleshy with rich, ripe, redcurrant and dark cherry flavours and a neat balance between the fruit and tannins on the finish. Not a keeper but delightful current drinking.

1998 Rothbury Mudgee Shiraz $12.95

Although Rothbury is a Hunter Valley winery and part of the Fosters–Mildara Blass empire, this hearty red comes from the company's Mudgee vineyards. It has some brambly, ripe dark plum and spice flavours, is rich, deep and satisfying with a smooth texture and pleasing finish.

1998 Seppelt Terrain Shiraz ☆ $12.00

This is a very impressive quaffer that we believe represents excellent value for money. It has rich, concentrated, ripe, dark plum flavours, some juiciness, fleshy texture, good weight and substantial yet fine tannins.

1998 Stonehaven Shiraz $14.95

Another outstanding red from the BRL Hardy portfolio, this time from their new, state-of-the-art Stonehaven winery close to the town of Padthaway. This is a blend of shiraz from different parts of the Limestone Coast: Padthaway (75 per cent), Coonawarra (18 per cent) and Wrattonbully (7 per cent). It has a deep, inky colour, smoky, plummy aromas, rich, ripe, concentrated dark plum flavours, vibrant juicy fruit, and fine ripe tannins. There is impressive complexity and weight, good balance between oak and fruit and above all a delicious ripeness. Great vintage, excellent value.

1999 Swanbrook Premium Classic Red $13.95

In spite of the label, this is a 100 per cent shiraz made from 62-year-old vines at the original Gnangara Vineyard at Henley Brook. While the sweet coconutty vanillin oak dominates the nose and the palate, it does have some ripe blackberry and chocolate flavours and a soft texture.
Limited availability all states except SA. Call (08) 92963100 or email swanbrookwines@optusnet.com.au

1997 The Wine Society St Halletts Shiraz $14.45

A very impressive offering from the Wine Society. Made by St Halletts from Barossa Valley fruit, this is a dense, brooding beauty with intense, blackberry, dark plum and cedary oak characters, smooth texture and a soft finish. A little oaky and one dimensional but with attractive flavours.
Available from the Wine Society. Call 1300 723 723 or email orders@winesociety.com.au

1998 Wyndham Estate Bin 555 Shiraz $10.95

The latest release of this old Hunter Valley favourite has ripe, almost jammy red berry fruit, well-integrated vanillin oak, good richness and concentration and an attractive supple finish. Good drinking, especially at the price.

2000 Yellow Tail Shiraz $9.95

Yet another label of Casella Wines and the best of the current release reds from this Griffith based producer. It is fresh, clean, juicy and light-bodied and has lovely red cherry perfumes, vibrant raspberry and redcurrant flavours. A triumph of the style.

CABERNET SAUVIGNON

Not surprisingly, the best examples that we found of the classic grape variety, cabernet sauvignon, are outstanding wines. The variety has done extraordinarily well in Australia, except in regions which are too cool to fully ripen it. Many of Australia's most expensive and most sought after reds are straight cabernets.

We are able to recommend some good examples of cabernet from the warmer, irrigated regions along the Murray and these tend to sell below $10. The best of the cabernet sauvignons from our tastings push close to the $15 price point, which is scarcely surprising as they are sourced from relatively low-yielding premium regions and, in some cases, are treated to expensive brand new oak and made using labour intensive methods.

Vintage does make a difference and quality does shift from year to year in Australia. Both the 1998 and 1999 vintages were outstanding in most parts of Australia and this is reflected in the wines we have recommended (13 out of about 50 tasted).

The great delight for both of us was the way in which the best cabernets we tasted—the Hardys Tintara Cellars, the McWilliams Coonawarra and the Orlando Jacob's Creek Reserve—appeared to be lifting the bar. By offering wines of such incredible quality at this price point, these three large companies appear to be suggesting that further improvement is possible and that to match them, other wineries will need to find ways to increase quality while keeping prices modest. Very good news indeed for quaffers.

O! Quaff! Award Winner   Best Buy   **M** Max's Pick   Peter's Pick

1998 Angove's Sarnia Farm Cabernet $14.95

Over the past five or six years, the Sarnia Farm has helped lift Angove's profile with Aussie wine lovers: it's a reasonably priced, quality cabernet from Padthaway. The 1998 vintage has yielded a stunner which we like much better than the cabernet from the previous vintage. This is an almost voluptuous red with fragrant vanillin oak aromas, dense blackcurrant and dark plum flavours and fine, quite gentle tannins. It is soft, round and lush with a velvety texture. Although the oak is quite bold, it is neatly integrated with the rich, concentrated fruit.

1999 Carramar Estate Cabernet $9.95

Carramar Estate is one of the labels of Casella, a progressive winery operating a state-of-the-art facility from Griffith in the Riverina. This is a well-priced wine: not as good as some of those that cost $5 more but fair value at under $10. It has scented red berry aromas, is supple and pleasant in the mouth with cedary oak, redcurrant and red cherry flavours and even a hint of tobacco. Sure, it's a bit firm and tannic on the finish, though that will probably improve if it has a few more months in the bottle, or if it's accompanied by osso buco or some full-flavoured meat dish.

1999 Deakin Estate Cabernet Sauvignon ⭐ $10.00

For a wine to be labelled cabernet sauvignon in Australia it must be made from at least 85 per cent of that variety. So, it's perfectly reasonable for this red to include pinot noir (3 per cent), ruby cabernet (3 per cent) and merlot (1 per cent) along with 93 per cent cabernet. It is sourced from near the Murray River at Red Cliffs, the Murray–Darling and north-western Victoria. This is a light, honest, direct style that is well-made, soft and appealing with red cherry flavours and some firmness on the finish.

1998 Hardys Tintara Cellars Cabernet Sauvignon
P M $14.50

We won't be surprised if some consumers confuse the Tintara Cellars wines with the $35 McLaren Vale reds which BRL Hardy market under the Tintara label: the packaging appears remarkably similar and the distinguishing word 'Cellars' is in the smallest print. Pity too because the Tintara Cellars range is fabulous news for the average punter and pushes the notion of what is possible for just under $15 to new limits. Winemakers Stephen Pannell and Simon White have sourced fruit from the McLaren Vale, Coonawarra and the Adelaide Hills, have used labour intensive techniques such as open fermentation and basket pressing and have matured the wine in 30 per cent new French and American oak barriques. Luxury.

This impressive red is powerful, opulent and deeply flavoured. Look for dark fruit and charry oak aromas, ripe plum, allspice and dark chocolate and vanillin oak characters on a silky smooth palate. The oak is overt at present but expect this to soften with some time in bottle. All in all, this is a terrific wine which Max thought 'very smart' and Peter supported for its 'elegance and concen-tration of sweet fruit flavours'.

1998 Lindemans Bin 45 Cabernet Sauvignon
☆ $9.50

Well, we do know how the folks at Lindemans do it (see the feature on blending Bin 65 on pages 67–69) but we agree it's hard to believe. This is a large volume red that sells heaps to the Americans, the British and plenty of others overseas and there's still enough available for Aussies who want a reasonable quality quaffer under $10. The grapes come mostly from Coonawarra, the Riverland and the Barossa Valley and there is some ruby cabernet and cabernet franc to flesh out the cabernet sauvignon. This is a lively and direct style: bright and purple in colour, fresh, ripe, red berry flavours with a firm, oaky finish. As Max says: 'light and bouncy'.

1998 McWilliams Coonawarra Cabernet Sauvignon
$14.95

This new regional range of McWilliams has been a source of delight for both of us. Chief Winemaker Jim Brayne has invested much time and effort into the McWilliams' operation in Coonawarra which has centred around revitalising the Brands label since the takeover. Brayne's task has been made much easier as he is able to count on the expertise and local knowledge of people like Brands' winemaker, Jim Brand. There is clever winemaking at play here too. After fermentation, the wine spends between nine and 15 days in new and one-year-old American and French barrels to give it an oak lift. After that it spends 18 months in older American (60 per cent) and French oak before being blended and bottled. A very impressive cabernet for this price bracket with the key word in both our tasting notes being 'restrained'. The wine has some spicy perfumes, refined red cherry, mulberry and mint flavours, a supple, smooth texture and fine gentle tannins to finish. It is elegant, medium-bodied and generous.

1998 Orlando Jacob's Creek Reserve Cabernet Sauvignon $14.95

We are impressed; so much so that if we were hat wearers we would be dipping our lids to Phil Laffer and the team at Orlando. The Jacob's Creek Reserve range is a triumph. With the Reserve Cabernet, the fruit has come in from premium regions—Coonawarra (49 per cent), Barossa (16 per cent), McLaren Vale (15 per cent), Padthaway (15 per cent) and Langhorne Creek (5 per cent)—and has been picked and vinified as separate parcels. Careful monitoring of quality continues until the decision is made whether or not to include individual barrels in the final blend. This is a powerful, full-bodied cabernet with vanillin oak and blackberry perfumes, brambly, blackcurrant flavours and substantial though fine tannins on a lingering finish. Max enjoyed its 'lean savoury characters' while Peter loved its 'opulence, depth and purity of fruit'.

1999 Rosemount Cabernet Sauvignon $14.95

Grapes for the Diamond Label Cabernet come mainly from company vineyards at Langhorne Creek and McLaren Vale with a smaller amount from Mudgee. Vinification focused on producing an approachable, early drinking style but with adequate concentration of flavour. While we both thought this wine was worth recommending, Max found it 'fairly simple, direct and plain, lacking oomph'. Peter saw it in a different line up where it stood out from the crowd for its immediate appeal and drinkability. It has ripe, redcurrant characters, is fleshy with clean, lively flavours and a soft, gentle finish.

1998 Seppelt Terrain Cabernet
⭐ **$12.00**

While not in the class of the 1998 Terrain Shiraz, this is still a pretty handy red at a reasonable price. Restrained red berry aromas, supple, smooth texture with redcurrant and dark chocolate flavours. It's a bit grippy on the finish and so you'll enjoy it much better with food. Think quality sausages and roast vegetables.

1998 Springbetts Cabernet Sauvignon
$14.95

This wine has been made for Cellarmasters by Grant Burge and celebrates some of his ancestors. It is made from Barossa Valley grapes and was partially barrel fermented and matured in new American oak. While this deep, vibrant red won't appeal to everyone—for some it will appear a bit chippy (read too oaky) and a bit heavy on the tannins—it does have plummy vanillin oak aromas, succulent ripe blackberry and dark plum flavours and is quite mellow. For those who like their oak heavy, it'll be a treat especially with a hearty T-bone steak, a concentrated red wine sauce and chips— with a healthy green salad to follow.
Available from Cellarmasters: call 1800 500 260 or visit www.cellarmasters.com.au

1999 Taylors Cabernet Sauvignon
$14.95

Taylors are the Clare Valley's largest producer and their wines have shown significant improvement in the past couple of vintages. This is an appealing cabernet that has richness and concentration and yet has the softness and fleshiness to make it excellent current drinking. Max liked its 'good toasty oak flavours, ripe raspberry and blackberry fruit and regional Clare earthy, resiny character,' while Peter enjoyed 'its attractive, coconutty vanillin oak, lush texture, good weight and soft, gentle finish'.

1998 Wolf Blass Eaglehawk Cabernet Sauvignon
$13.50

The Eaglehawk Cabernet is a powerful, full-bodied red with blackcurrant, dark cherry and smokey oak flavours, a lively, chewy texture and firmish, fine tannins on a persistent, long finish. Expect some softening with six to 12 months bottle age; otherwise, enjoy it with a beef or lamb roast.

1998 Wyndham Estate Bin 444 Cabernet Sauvignon
$10.95

This is a soft, sweet-fruited, easy-drinking red with ripe, red cherry and plummy flavours and a silky texture. The acids are quite high on the finish which some will find a tad off-putting although we expect these to soften with time. A crowd pleaser.

MERLOT

Merlot is only a fairly recent arrival on the Australian wine scene. Unlike shiraz and, to a lesser extent, cabernet sauvignon, merlot was not one of the varieties planted by Australia's early settler-vignerons. It wasn't until the 1970s and 1980s, when so-called 'Bordeaux blends' became popular among winemakers, that merlot was planted with any conviction (cabernet and merlot are the two main grapes in red Bordeaux).

Despite its recent arrival, though, merlot has become a firm favourite with winemakers and drinkers—at both ends of the price spectrum. Without anybody quite knowing how, merlot has gained a reputation in the popular consciousness as a producer of 'soft' wines—and a lot of people like their reds soft.

In cooler climate, premium wine districts, serious winemakers are chasing the big, oaky, plush, expensive style of merlot, exploiting the variety's supple tannin and plummy fruit characters. Ironically, it's precisely the same characteristics that many producers in the warmer districts are after to make much cheaper, everyday quaffing reds—the kind we're after, in other words.

We were pleased to find eight recommendable merlots, but bearing in mind that over half of them were the first or second vintage of a new brand, we suspect that we will see an onslaught of quaffing merlot over the next few years. And while it's early days, and producers are still working on how best to treat the variety, we would recommend drinking most cheap Australian merlot young and fresh, while its bright red fruit flavours are at their most vibrant.

 Quaff! Award Winner   Best Buy   Max's Pick   Peter's Pick

2000 Deakin Estate Merlot
P M ⭐ **$9.95**

Ever since it was launched about five years ago, the Deakin Estate publicity and advertising has promoted the image of laid-back, easy-going, worry-free wine enjoyment. For once, there's substance behind the hype, because the Deakin wines, always released young and bursting with fruit flavour, really do tend to provide an easy, attractive mouthful of enjoyment. This is packed with bright, ripe red fruit flavour—raspberries, cherries, plums—but is light and soft to finish. Good reliable value.

1999 Deakin Estate Select Merlot
$13.00

From the new Select range of varietal wines introduced by Deakin Estate to replace the slightly more expensive Alfred range, this (not surprisingly) has similar vibrant cherry and plum fruit flavours to the 'standard' Deakin merlot, but is slightly fuller-bodied and has an extra layer of flavours as well—smoky, biscuity characters—from the extra oak maturation it received.

1999 Hardys Regional Reserve Merlot
⭐ **$6.95**

This is a new—and very welcome—addition to the ultra-cheap RR range from Hardys. It's sourced from vineyards across south-eastern Australia, and is produced in substantial volume, hence the price. The wine has a kind of subtitle on the label — 'soft dry red'—and we can't argue with that: it's certainly soft, round and light, but there's also far more bright, ripe berry and currant flavour than you'd expect at this price level. Great value, easy-drinking pizza red.

1998 James Busby Merlot
$13.99

Named rather grandly after the 'founding father' of Australian viticulture (Busby imported hundreds of different vine varieties, planted a vineyard in the Hunter Valley and wrote manuals on grape-growing and winemaking), this is far from a grand wine. In fact it's downright humble. It's a Barossa merlot made exclusively for Liquorland by Grant Burge, and it has the region and the winemaker stamped all over it: ripe, plump, bramble fruit wrapped up in a blanket of sweet, smoky oak. Good, fun, barbecue merlot for people who like their wine full-bodied.
Available through Liquorland and Vintage Cellars.

1999 Jindalee Merlot
$13.95

Jindalee burst onto the scene only a couple of years ago with bright, impressive sun-filled wines in bright, impressive, sun-filled packaging. The Riverland-based company has hundreds of hectares of grapes in the Murray Darling region, and is able to keep prices very competitive. While we were less impressed by Jindalee's other reds, we liked the merlot: it has a fair amount of obvious vanilla flavour, thanks to the American oak maturation, but there's plenty of ripe, velvety, plummy-rich fruit to back it up.

1999 Mount Pleasant Hunter Valley Merlot
$14.95

A great example of the region dominating the variety and the winemaking. While this lovely merlot has all the plummy roundness you'd expect from the variety, and some good, savoury oak, the main flavour seems to be an attractive, dark earthiness which we taste a lot in red wines from the Hunter. We also tasted the 1998 vintage of this wine, and found it had cleaner, less regional plush, plummy fruit flavours, with some stylish savoury oak balancing the sweetness. Both are good, and both (according to McWilliams) are available—the 1998 in more limited quantities, obviously.

1998 Normans White Label Merlot $14.95

This wine may not appeal to all tastes. It has a herbal, slightly green pepper character which some might associate with slightly unripe grapes, but we are inclined to think it is a valid varietal flavour of merlot—we think it's more attractively herbal than green. We like the wine most, though, for its light, very pleasant, juicy palate. A very easy-drinking wine.

1999 Rosemount Estate Diamond Label Merlot $14.95

Another new wine. Although Rosemount have made a Diamond Label merlot for years, it's been for export eyes only. In 1999, though, they had enough fruit from their South Australia and New South Wales vineyards to make more—and sell it locally. We're happy they did, because this is a good wine: some well-handled smoky oak flavours support a medium-full but soft palate of round, plummy fruit, enhanced by a hint of merlot's herbal aromatic quality.

OTHER RED VARIETALS

There is, of course, much more to life than shiraz, cabernet sauvignon, merlot and grenache—although the way these four red grapes dominate the Australian wine scene, you could be forgiven for thinking otherwise. The wine world is home to thousands of different red varieties, and while not all of them are planted in Australia—and only a handful are considered 'premium' enough to bother with in the first place—there are plenty out there that offer different taste experiences from the mainstream and are worth seeking out if you're feeling adventurous.

There are two problems with finding 'other' red varietal wines under $15. In the case of pinot noir, for example, the problem is that the grape variety likes to be grown in a cool climate, it needs to be cropped at a fairly low level to ensure quality and it needs sensitive handling in the winery—all of which costs money. This in turn leads to a high price tag. We were rather pleased, then—and surprised—to find a solid five under $15 pinots to recommend. On the other hand, varieties like malbec and durif are generally considered by winemakers to be second-rate varieties and can, as a result, receive second-rate treatment in the vineyards and winery—a self-fulfilling prophesy of mediocrity, if you like. The wines we recommend have obviously been made by winemakers who are gunning for the underdogs.

On a final note, we believe that as demand and competition increase at the bottom end of the red wine market and producers (and consumers) continue to look for points of difference, the choice of other red varietals will also grow. It won't be too long before we see cheap Australian-made sangiovese, tempranillo, barbera and more hitting the bottle shop shelves. So watch this space—and roll on diversity.

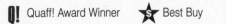 Quaff! Award Winner Best Buy Max's Pick Peter's Pick

pinot noir

1999 Barak's Bridge Pinot Noir
P $13.95

As we've said, finding good pinot noir under $15 is hard; finding pinot noir from one of the Yarra Valley's top producers with complex smells of top-quality French barrels for under $15, is next to impossible. But that's what this wine, the second label of Yering Station winery, manages to offer. The fruit is perhaps just a little on the light and short side (pinot noir at this price level is seldom going to be anything but light-bodied) but the toasty, smoky barrel smells are just so seductive that you'd almost forgive the wine anything. Drink with barbecued quail, or simple roast chook. Yum.

1999 De Bortoli Windy Peak Pinot Noir
$13.00

A consistently good pinot in the under $15 category. This is another second label from a Yarra Valley winery, although this time it is made in much larger quantities using grapes sourced from across Victoria. This wine is all about fruit: lively raspberry and strawberry fruit, simple but direct and juicy right across the tongue. Although the wine's good to quaff right now, we also suspect six months to a year might see some complex, earthy characters begin to creep in.

1999 Lindemans Bin 99 Pinot Noir
$9.50

Ridiculously good value. Okay, so this is not earth-shatteringly complex or deep, or rich, but it's got good, honest strawberry and cherry flavours, is well-made, balanced and finishes soft and fine. A good introduction to the uncomplicated joy of pinot noir for anyone who's never tried the variety before and is perhaps a little tired of heavy, oaky shiraz.

1999 Rosemount Estate Diamond Label Pinot Noir
$14.95

Is there a grape variety that Philip Shaw and the winemaking team at Rosemount don't know how to make well? We're yet to find it. This wine is quite dark-coloured, spicy and plummy-flavoured, with a firmness and fuller body than the other pinots in this price bracket. Not that we're complaining—these characters would make it an ideal candidate for robust pasta dishes.

1999 Taylors Pinot Noir
$14.95

When we tasted this in August, we really fell for its incredibly youthful, bright purple cherry and raspberry fruit juiciness. But we also found the wine to be a bit unsettled—there was some dissolved carbon dioxide gas in the wine, as though it had just been bottled, which gave it a little spritz on the tongue. We figure that by the time you taste it, though, that youthful spritz will have calmed down.

malbec

1999 Bleasedale Malbec
$13.95

Malbec originated in south-west France and is one of the minor grapes used in the red wines of Bordeaux. It has been a fairly popular blending grape in Australian winemaking for decades, but rarely gets a chance to shine on its own as a varietal wine. Here it has been used to make a good, solid, vibrant young red that possibly displays a little more winery and regional character than varietal personality—it has rich minty, coconutty oak smells and is ripe, sweet, soft and fleshy in the mouth.

1999 McGuigan Limited Release Malbec Bin 5000 $11.99

Don't let the words 'limited release' fool you, there should be plenty of this wine around—until people realise what good value it is at $12 and snap it all up. This has a little more of the varietal malbec character we'd expect—a spicy, earthy, berry/minty flavour—and is seductively sweet, round and mellow in the mouth. Easy-drinking red wine.

durif

1999 Mirrool Creek Durif M ⭐ $8.99

Durif originated in the south of France, and is grown fairly extensively in two areas of Australia: north-east Victoria and, for this wine, in the Riverina in New South Wales. Durif has a reputation for producing dark, dense, earthy, big-bodied red wine and this one, released under Miranda's revamped and smartened-up Mirrool Creek label, is no exception. Intense black–purple in colour, it is bursting with tarry fruit and smoky oak smells and is heroically proportioned in the mouth, with firm tannins and a tongue-hugging grip. For lovers of big, brawny, slightly old-fashioned red wine. A real surprise.

tarrango

**2000 Brown Brothers
Tarrango
$12.50**

Tarrango is a grape variety proudly developed by Australia's own CSIRO specifically to make light red wine under local conditions, and its commercial production is pretty much limited to Brown Brothers in north-east Victoria. This couldn't be any further from the Mirrool Creek Durif in style—it's pale-looking, light scarlet in colour, has gentle smells of summer strawberries and is delicate, juicy, lively and very light in the mouth. Drink very young, perhaps chilled like a rosé, during summer.

CABERNET MERLOT BLENDS

This blending of two classic red grape varieties makes one of the world's great wine styles and is now found in most parts of the globe where vineyards flourish. At its best, the power and tight structure of the cabernet are fleshed out by the richness and lush texture of the merlot to make a harmonious, well-integrated blend.

The question of oak handling is crucial to the quality of these wines. Balance is the key: richer, more powerful fruit can handle newer, stronger oak flavours; light to medium bodied reds are best if complemented by gentle oak characters. Oak chips are necessarily and widely used with wines at these price points. Care needs to be exercised to avoid overt chippiness.

Most wines under $15 are made for immediate drinking. Of those recommended here (eight out of the 37 we tasted), the most impressive will improve with six to 12 months bottle age, while the 1998 Gramp's and the 1998 Lysander are likely to benefit from being well stored for three to five years.

 Quaff! Award Winner   ★ Best Buy   M Max's Pick   P Peter's Pick

1998 Andrew Garrett Cabernet Merlot $14.95

Charles Hargrave is making some excellent wines at the $14 price point for this Mildara Blass-owned McLaren Vale producer. We're impressed with the versatility of the Andrew Garrett team and are happy to recommend five out of six wines submitted for *Quaff!* An excellent result. This red is a blend of cabernet (90 per cent) and merlot (10 per cent) from Padthaway (74 per cent) and McLaren Vale (26 per cent) which has been aged in new and older American and French hogsheads for 15 months. It is a big, full-bodied, powerful red with some red berry and vanillin oak aromas, a supple, silky texture, and good, deep redcurrant, red cherry, juicy fruit under the oak and tannin. Quite tight and firm but with plenty of rich fruit to maintain reasonable balance.

1998 Gramp's Cabernet Merlot P M $14.95

Only the largest companies can blend as extensively as this to produce large volumes of a wine. With this potent red, the cabernet comes from Padthaway, the Barossa, McLaren Vale and Clare while the merlot is sourced from McLaren Vale, Mudgee and Padthaway. Care is taken with the oak treatment too: the more robust cabernet was aged in new and one-year-old French oak while the more elegant cabernet and the merlot was matured in older French and American oak. Attention to detail is one of Chief Winemaker Phil Laffer's bywords and each barrel is tasted before being included in the blend. Big, rich, concentrated and powerful—that sums it up. On the nose, it is dense and brooding while on the palate you have masses of intense black fruit wrapped in quite firm oak and ripe sweet tannins. This is a full-bodied, velvety red with impressive weight and the ability to improve with cellaring. It'll be at its best with bold flavours: sirloin steak with mushroom, fried onions and mash or, better still, wait a while and serve it with a wintery casserole of ox-tail or lamb shanks.

1998 Haselgrove Sovereign Cabernet Merlot
⭐ $10.95

At this price it's scarcely surprising that the grapes are sourced predominantly from the Haselgrove vineyards on the Riverland. There is, however, a small amount of fruit that has come from the McLaren Vale and the Limestone Coast. It is a light- to medium-bodied red with minty aromas, juicy, plummy, flavours and a soft, clean finish. Max sees the slightest hint of green fruit, but we both believe that the Sovereign Cab Merlot is bright, vibrant and fruity enough for that not to be noticed.

1999 Kingston Estate Cabernet Merlot
$12.95

While the year 2000 has been a fairly tough one for the Riverland producer, it's fair to say that this is the kind of rich, full-flavoured cabernet blend that has given the Australian wine industry a good name. The grapes come from quite low yielding vineyards in the Riverland and the King Valley. The 1999 Kingston Cabernet Merlot is very fine with deep, dark red fruit flavours, silky, fleshy texture and ripe, firmish tannins.

1998 Lysander
Cabernet Sauvignon
Merlot
$14.99

Heads are being turned by the quality of the reds coming from Mt Benson on South Australia's Limestone Coast. Factor in the fair price of this beauty from the Cellarmasters portfolio and you have two very good reasons to purchase. The 1998 Lysander red has deep, ripe purple fruit, dark cherry and toasty oak aromas, is supple, vibrant and full-flavoured with some dark chocolate, dark plums and licorice characters, good weight and neat balance. It is tight and firm without being aggressive. A stylish red.

Available from Cellarmasters: call 1800 500 260 or visit www.cellarmasters.com.au

1998 Orlando Triology
Cabernet Sauvignon
Cabernet Franc Merlot
$13.95

Another impressive red from Orlando Wyndham, this time a trio of the grape varieties that have made Bordeaux famous—cabernet sauvignon, cabernet franc and merlot. It is predominantly sourced from Coonawarra and Padthaway in one of their best ever vintages. This is an elegant red: some leafy fragrance, red cherry, plummy flavours, supple texture and medium weight with good balance between the fruit and the tannins.

2000 Rosemount Estate
Cabernet Merlot
⭐$ $11.95

This is the latest of the Rosemount Split Label reds which consistently prove to be among the most impressive Aussie reds in their price bracket. Peter loved this one for 'its supple, silky smooth texture, red cherry and spice flavours and soft gentle finish' while Max enjoyed its 'fragrant varietal cabernet fruit, its polished sweet red berry fruit balanced by a touch of leanness'.

1998 Wyndham Estate Bin 888 Cabernet Merlot $12.95

This is the quintessential quaffer: good, bright, intense spicy, redcurrant, red cherry, plummy flavours, fleshy texture and ripe, sweet tannins with some power. Max wrote about its 'lovely core of soft sweetness' and when the wine's identity was revealed, remembered an earlier comment on obvious sweetness in the Bin 555 Shiraz. Most importantly, the Bin 888 is neatly balanced having sufficient rich fruit and tannin to balance any sweetness. It's flavoursome and easy to drink.

SHIRAZ CABERNET BLENDS

If we had to nominate the archetypal, everyday Australian quaffing red—the wine we instinctively reach for on our way out to a barbecue—it would probably be the classic blend of shiraz and cabernet sauvignon. The warm, round, generous flavours of the shiraz grape just meld so well with the firmer, tighter, more structured flavours of the cabernet, with the result (when it's good) often being an incredibly satisfying glassful of red.

No other wine producing country in the world puts these two varieties together as often as Australia; indeed, in France where both varieties come from, the idea of putting shiraz (from the Rhône Valley) together with cabernet (from Bordeaux, hundreds of kilometres away) is positively frowned upon by the authorities.

In many ways, the blend came about in Australia by historical accident. In the early days, producers found that shiraz on its own could often taste a bit too soft and round, that it needed something to give it backbone and firmness in the mouth. They also discovered that cabernet sauvignon could often be a bit too firm and tough on its own, that it needed something blended with it to soften it out. The solution was obvious: a little bit of shiraz in with the cabernet, and vice versa, and Bob's your uncle—a more complete wine.

Over the last couple of decades, there has been a shift away from shiraz cabernet as a premium wine style ('premium' as in bottles over $15), with producers favouring single varietal wines or more 'classic' (read pseudo-European) blends like cabernet with merlot (the Bordeaux model) or shiraz with grenache (the Rhône Valley model). Don't worry, because our tastings revealed that down in the quaffing end of the price spectrum (the real world) there's still plenty of great shiraz cabernet to be found.

 Quaff! Award Winner Best Buy Max's Pick Peter's Pick

1998 Andrew Garrett Shiraz Cabernet Franc $14.50

Andrew Garrett (the winemaker, the man) no longer has anything to do with the Andrew Garrett brand (it's owned by Mildara Blass) but the bold styles of wine he established under his own name are still very much what you can expect from this label. This wine has a good, deep purple colour, some full, nutty oak and bramble fruit smells and quite a firm, tannic impression in the mouth. The cabernet franc grape variety is similar to cabernet sauvignon, but is a little finer, more fragrant, with a slightly tighter structure.

Non Vintage Banrock Station Shiraz Cabernet ☆ $6.95

This is neither the first nor the only Banrock Station wine to appear in this book—we are very impressed with the consistency and value for money of this brand. This shiraz cabernet is precisely the kind of easy, bright red, juicy raspberry and vanilla flavoured everyday quaffing wine you want for seven bucks a bottle. It's also, interestingly, a non-vintage wine (i.e. a blend of more than one year) which should help ensure consistency of style and quality.

1998 Bastion Shiraz Cabernet $14.00

A new and very welcome label from the historic Leasingham winery in South Australia's Clare Valley, designed, we assume, to fill the gap left by the winery's long-running Bin 56 cabernet malbec and Bin 61 shiraz, which are now both over $15 (unfortunately). This wine manages to provide heaps of regional red wine personality along with terrific value. Dark, full of minty purple berry fruit flavour and smoky oak, it has the kind of firm, rather robust, full-bodied structure that either suggests drinking now with rare steak or stashing under the bed for a couple of years to mellow. A big, bold wine.

1998 Bleasedale Potts Family Shiraz Cabernet $13.95

The Potts family recently celebrated a very impressive 150 years of winemaking at their Bleasedale winery in Langhorne Creek. Rather generous of them, then, to sell a wine named in their collective multi-generational honour for a mere fourteen bucks. Then again, the great value of Bleasedale red wines has been a bit of a badly-kept secret for a while...guess the secret's out now, though! This wine is for lovers of sweetly oaky, very ripe, hedonistic South Australian red wine: it's like diving into a lamington, with flavours of rich chocolate, coconutty oak and a soft, round, comforting texture. If you like that style, you'll love this.

1998 Elderton Tantalus Shiraz Cabernet $13.95

Elderton's premium wines—especially the expensive and sought-after Command shiraz—are well known for being almost exaggerated expressions of Barossa Valley red, with ultra-ripe, sometimes jammy fruit and stacks and stacks of toasty, smoky, vanilla oak. The more accessibly-priced Tantalus blend is, thankfully, also a little more accessible as a drink. Sure, there's an obvious vanilla oakiness to the flavours, but it's nicely in balance with the medium- to full-bodied bramble fruit also running through the wine. A good barbecue quaffer with sausages and grainy mustard.

1999 Fox River Shiraz Cabernet
Q! P M $14.95

Fox River is the second label of Mount Barker winery, Goundrey, one of Western Australia's largest producers. While not all the wines in the Fox River range impressed us, this wine knocked our socks off. It's a fine, medium-bodied, focussed red wine which couldn't be further in style from the rich, oaky, full-bodied blockbusters coming out of South Australia. Even though a third of the grapes that went into it in fact came from South Australia, the two-thirds Western Australian, cooler climate fruit really dominates, giving the wine a vibrant, peppery, spicy, intense dark juiciness. Really quite excellently drinkable, even at this young age, and very good indeed.

1999 Geoff Merrill Cabernet Shiraz
$14.95

Geoff Merrill is one of the wine industry's great characters, with his David Boon look-alike moustache and wicked sense of humour. He's also a well-respected winemaker and although we've found some of his red wines a little lacking in oomph over the years, we liked this young, bouncy bold red a lot. It has a great glowing purple colour, a lifted aroma of dark blackberry fruit and an attractive earthiness running through the firm, full-bodied palate. The cabernet is the dominant partner in the blend and you can really taste it—the wine is a little firmer than many other blends we're recommending here.

1999 Jacob's Creek Shiraz Cabernet
⭐ **$8.95**

You'll find the whole story of this classic quaffer on pages 164–166. Is it our imagination, or does the price of Jacob's Creek seem to be going backwards? Perhaps the rest of the market is just creeping up slowly, because when we found out the recommended retail price of this wine we were more than pleasantly surprised—and you may be able to find it for less, which makes it even better value. It's all about immediate pleasure: good, bright, soft raspberry fruit backed up by just enough toasty oak flavour to give it interest and life. Good, honest drinking—which is exactly as it should be.

1998 Koonunga Hill Shiraz Cabernet
$12.90

Drinking Koonunga Hill from a good vintage is like catching up with an old friend: it just has the kind of satisfying, familiar character about it that makes you sit and linger with a bottle, waffling on for hours. And the 1998 vintage was a good one for South Australia (which is where most of the fruit for this huge blend comes from) so we weren't surprised to find this on top form: it's a great black red colour, with dark, dense, full-bodied bramble fruit and sweet oak flavours. Very good now, we also reckon five or even ten years in a cool, dark place will turn this into a magical wine.

1998 Maiden Gully Shiraz Cabernet $14.95

A brand new label from Balgownie Estate in the Bendigo region of central Victoria. Balgownie has a proud 30-year history of making some very impressive, full-bodied wines from shiraz and cabernet that take years to soften; this new wine is a much more accessible, easy-drinking red made as a blend of the two. Bright purple in the glass, it has fairly concentrated, plush, bramble fruit and sweet oak richness, like the traditional Balgownie wines, but there's a liveliness and spiciness to it that makes it highly enjoyable as a youngster.

1998 Metala Shiraz Cabernet $14.95

Just as we were writing the final words of this book in September, the results of the International Wine Challenge were announced in London with the 1998 Metala named as one of three Red Wine of the Year trophy winners—an incredible result. The competition is the world's largest, with over 9000 wines entered. It's fully deserved, too—this is simply a great quaffing wine, with dark, bold, ripe black fruit and smoky oak flavours running through a full, well-balanced, lovely round palate. Great red wines have been produced under the Metala label for decades—indeed, the better wines can develop in the bottle for decades. This vintage does the name proud.

1998 Rohrlach Barossa Valley Cabernet Shiraz $14.95

This is one of the best wines we've tasted from the extensive Cellarmasters range, a really powerful mouthful of Barossa Valley red wine that could easily be sold for ten dollars more. The wine is sourced from a well-established Barossa grape-growing family (the Rohrlachs) and shows all the hallmarks of the warm region and warm vintage—it's a big, bold drink, full of ripe blackberry fruit and spicy, toasty oak. The cabernet dominance makes itself felt in the wine's firm, lingering backbone. **Available through Cellarmasters: call 1800 500 260 or visit www.cellarmasters.com.au**

2000 Rosemount Estate Split Label Shiraz Cabernet ▯! ☆ $11.95

For the last two or three years, it's been a tussle between which of the two shiraz blends released in Rosemount's Split Label series is the better: the shiraz cabernet, or the grenache shiraz. We're tussling again this year, with Max leaning more towards the latter and Peter more towards this wine, with its bright purple colour, its sweet-tasting, silky-smooth berry fruit flavours and its soft, round, juicy finish. Whichever way you look at it, though, it's sensational value—especially at its regularly advertised price of $10 or under.

1998 Seppelt Moyston Cabernet Shiraz ☆ $7.80

The Moyston label has been associated with Seppelt's Great Western winery in Victoria for decades (it's the name of an old vineyard near the very small town of Moyston) and at one time was the source of some very fine wines indeed. Today, the name is on thousands and thousands of cases of good value wines sourced from across south-eastern Australia. Impeccably made, with a lick of vanilla oak flavour supporting some juicy medium-weight berry fruit, this is an easy, drink-now style of red at a good price.

1999 Spires Shiraz Cabernet
⭐ **$9.95**

The Spires range is a relatively new line-up from BRL Hardy focussing on the flavours and wine styles of the Barossa Valley. While not, perhaps, as full-on Barossa in style as we may have liked (in other words, it could have had a bit more depth and grunt), it's still a very attractive, bright, berry-fruity red wine with a highly gluggable juiciness.

1999 Taylors Promised Land Shiraz Cabernet
$13.95

The normal Taylors labels—plain, old-fashioned, rather daggy—would be familiar to most Australian wine drinkers and would probably represent cosy reliability. Bearing this in mind, Taylors have created a decidedly more modern label to accompany new introductions to the range such as this excellent shiraz cabernet—it's certainly not intended to be a cheaper or second brand, as the price is hardly any different. This is a remarkably approachable and enjoyable red wine with rich, ripe purple fruit, very mellow, round oak flavours and a well-balanced, lingering finish.

Classic quaffers

JACOB'S CREEK SHIRAZ CABERNET

It's not every day you get to do a vertical tasting of Jacob's Creek. Vertical tastings (where you compare the same wine over a number of vintages) are usually reserved for auspicious, serious, flagship wines like Grange and Hill of Grace, not $9 quaffing brands that sell millions of cases around the world each year.

And yet here we are, standing in the tasting room at Orlando's huge Barossa Valley winemaking headquarters, and lined up on the bench in front of us are five vintages of Jacob's Creek shiraz cabernet. There are tastings of Orlando's other wines, too—more expensive, premium numbers like Steingarten riesling, St Hugo cabernet, Lawson's shiraz—but it's the Jacob's Creek that we're intrigued by. Because when you think about it, for countless people across the globe Jacob's Creek is Australia's flagship wine.

Orlando's chief winemaker, Philip Laffer, is an industry veteran with 45 years experience behind him. His main winemaking principle is a bold and controversial one: 'I think people drink style more than they drink quality and if you as a winemaker forget that then you've lost them. If you diverge from your style, at the bottom level you lose the wine consumer because your wine is different—and Jacob's Creek drinkers notice when the style of their wine changes, believe me.'

So although the Jacob's Creek shiraz cabernet has changed over the last few vintages—moving away from using bags of oak chips towards using whole oak staves inside the tanks of fermenting and maturing wine, to impart oak flavour—the change has been one that has affected quality rather than style. The so-called 'plank tank technology' gives the wine a more integrated, less coarse oak flavour than the chips. The blend, roughly two-thirds shiraz to one-third cabernet, and the fruit flavours have stayed pretty much the same. This dedication to getting the style right is one of the reasons why Jacob's Creek shiraz cabernet has been able to maintain such a strong position for so long—and in the cut-throat world of wine marketing, any brand that lasts for longer than 10 years is an unqualified legend.

The first vintage of this now-classic quaffer was in 1973 and it was part of a range of wines named after Orlando-owned vineyards in the Barossa Valley (none of the other labels have survived). The Jacob's Creek name itself comes from the small trickle that runs past the original winery and vineyard established by Orlando's founder, Johann Gramp, in 1847. Although much of the fruit for the early Jacob's Creek wines did indeed come from the Barossa—shiraz, cabernet and, for the first 20 years, some malbec too—when the brand took off in export markets in the late 1980s and went through an enormous growth phase, the net was cast ever further.

Today, to make the two million plus cases of Jacob's Creek shiraz cabernet that Orlando do annually, about 50 per cent of the fruit comes from the inland irrigated regions such as the Riverland and Sunraysia, with the rest being sourced from Orlando's huge vineyards in Langhorne Creek, McLaren Vale, Padthaway and other premium districts.

For many in the industry, though, it's Jacob's Creek's success in export markets that is the main measure of its success. It took off in the UK about 10 years ago—many still remember the sight of London's red double decker buses emblazoned with the words 'Jacob's Creek: Australia's Top Drop'—and the brand is credited with leading Australia's incredible growth in that market. Indeed, Jacob's

Creek is now the number one wine brand in the UK, full stop, and is the only wine brand (as opposed to a human being) to have been awarded the prestigious Maurice O'Shea Award.

As we've mentioned elsewhere in this book, we are also very impressed with the new extension to the Jacob's Creek range—the Reserves—the reds especially. Although they're still under $15, they are a big step up in quality and achieve Phil Laffer's aim of building on the credibility of one of Australia's great wine success stories.

OTHER RED BLENDS

The majority of red blends available on the market fit into the traditional Australian styles—shiraz cabernet, cabernet merlot or grenache blends—so this chapter may appear to be a convenience for authors trying to cover all their bases, and so it is. Perhaps it's a little bit like many of these blends, which are the result of clever winemakers finding a home for unused batches of reasonable- to good-quality reds. When they are successful, this can result in unexpectedly good wines.

At the top end, with wines like the Russet Ridge, Rawsons Retreat, Jamiesons Run and the Sir James Red Blend, these are well-established brands with a loyal clientele. The regional and varietal composition is likely to vary depending on vintage conditions but these large companies work hard to maintain consistency of style.

Other reds here such as the Alkoomi, the Peel Estate, the Peter Lehmann and the Richmond Grove provide the punter with the opportunity to enjoy fruit sourced from premium regions at reasonable prices. There are also the very cheap wines from unfashionable regions where the winemakers have produced delightful red blends at unfashionable prices.

We did find examples of wines in this category where it appeared that convenience was the dominant motivation for the blend. As with elsewhere in this book, the best wines are worth seeking out.

 Quaff! Award Winner   ⭐ Best Buy   Max's Pick   Peter's Pick

1999 Alkoomi Mt Frankland Red $15.00

This is a straightforward, pleasant red from Alkoomi, which is based near Frankland in Western Australia's Great Southern. One of the region's pioneers and now a moderately large producer, Alkoomi has the economies of scale to make quality wines like this at reasonable prices. The 1999 Mt Frankland Red has delicate red berry perfumes, raspberry, redcurrant and plummy flavours, fleshy texture and softish tannins.

1999 Fiddleback ☆ $11.00

Fiddleback is a new venture into the world of modestly priced wines which appears likely to be a success for the Pyrenees producer, Taltarni. This soft, easy-drinking, light to medium-bodied red is fresh and vibrant, with raspberry and mulberry flavours, a silky texture and a clean, soft finish.

1999 Hardys Regional Reserve Shiraz Ruby Cabernet ☆ $6.95

This is a blend of shiraz and ruby cabernet from the Riverland in the RR (Regional Reserve) range for BRL Hardy. It is a simple, straight-forward quaffer that is soft, round and smooth with spicy, red berry flavours. Unpretentious but fair value at the price.

1998 Hardys Sir James Cab Shiraz Merlot $13.95

Another very good wine at the price from BRL Hardys Stephen Pannell, this is a blend of cabernet, shiraz and merlot from McLaren Vale and Langhorne Creek. It has quite subtle perfumes on the nose, is clean, fresh and bright, has red berry and plum flavours, tight structure and quite a tannic finish. Expect it to soften with six months to a year in the bottle, or enjoy it now with a rich, full-flavoured beef casserole.

1998 Jamiesons Run Coonawarra Dry Red $14.95

This is a regular favourite and one of the more consistent performers from Coonawarra at this price point. The 1998 is a blend of cabernet (80 per cent), shiraz (17 per cent) and merlot (3 per cent) from Mildara Blass's extensive vineyards in Coonawarra. In our tastings, it appeared as a good rather than a great Jamiesons Run. We found it a touch oaky on the nose with some ripe, red cherry flavours, a smooth texture and a pleasant, softish finish.

1999 McWilliams Inheritance Shiraz Merlot ◖! ☆ $6.95

Thank goodness for blind tastings. There are so few blendings of shiraz and merlot that it seems a strange mix—until you taste it. Both of us had raved about the wine but the retail price caused us to do a back flip; make that a double back flip. The Inheritance Shiraz Merlot is an amazing Riverina red that has lovely, vanillin oak aromas, is lively, bright and direct, rich and concentrated with a fleshy texture, some silkiness, red cherry and plum flavours and an attractive, supple finish.

1997 Orlando Russet Ridge Coonawarra Cabernet Sauvignon Shiraz Merlot P M $14.95

Three-year-old reds are rare finds in *Quaff!* and the additional bottle age certainly benefits this wine. While the 1997 vintage in Coonawarra did not reach the stellar heights of the vintages on either side of it, there is no question about its quality. This is a powerful, full-bodied red with ripe, redcurrant and plum characters, lush, fleshy texture, good richness, weight and depth of flavour and fine tannins on a pleasant, supple finish that lingers.

1999 Penfolds Rawsons Retreat Shiraz Cabernet Ruby Cabernet $10.00

The multi-regional Rawsons Retreat once again shows the depth of the Penfolds red portfolio. The 1999 blend has ripe, dark cherry and black plum flavours, a smooth texture, medium body and reasonable power. Good value.

1998 Queen Adelaide Regency Red ⭐ $7.00

This is a straightforward medium-bodied red with some terrific flavours—red berry perfumes, raspberry, red cherry flavours, a silky texture and a firmish finish.

1999 Peel Estate Pichet Red $14.95

Peel Estate is a small quality winery, established in 1974 by Will Nairn and still run by him on the coast plain at Baldivis, about 60 kilometres south of Perth. Pichet is the term used in France for the jug in which the house wine is served and the Peel Estate red is a blend of unoaked merlot and cabernet franc. While Max was less enthusiastic, Peter loved its light, bright, vibrant and lively flavours, ripe cassis aromas, squashy blackcurrant and dark plum characters and gentle, fine tannins.

1999 Peter Lehmann Clancy's Red Blend $13.95

Just as the presses started to roll, we managed to see the latest vintage of the Peter Lehmann red blend celebrating Banjo Patterson's famous poem and he of the Overflow. Shiraz, cabernet sauvignon, merlot and cabernet franc (from the Barossa, naturally) are blended to make a soft, fragrant, easy-drinking red with some style. The Clancy's Red has good structure, vibrant, clean, fresh red plum and cherry flavours and good length.

1999 Richmond Grove Cabernet Sauvignon Shiraz Merlot $10.95

This is a blend of cabernet (54 per cent), shiraz (30 per cent) and merlot (16 per cent) from five premium South Australian regions: Coonawarra, Padthaway, McLaren Vale, Clare and Barossa. It was aged in two- and three-year-old French and American oak for between six and nine months. This is quite a tightly structured, powerful, youthful red blend with some spice, redcurrant and eucalypt characters and a firm finish. There's no doubting its quality, though the wine could do with a bit more time to soften and fill out.

1999 Vintage Cellars Quaffing Dry Red ⭐ $7.69

This is a soft, round easy-drinking red that has some spicy, earthy, red berry flavours, a supple texture and a lively fresh finish. Good value.
Available through Vintage Cellars.

1998 Wolf Blass Eaglehawk Shiraz Merlot Cabernet Sauvignon $13.50

Another good Eaglehawk red from Chief Winemaker John Glaetzer and the Mildara Blass team. This shows powerful oak on the nose and palate but has the depth, richness and concentration of fruit to balance that. In the mid-palate it is soft and round and full-flavoured.

GRENACHE AND GRENACHE BLENDS

Grenache is its own worst enemy. The vine can—if it's left to its own devices—pump out huge crops of big-berried bunches of grapes, especially if it's grown in warm climates like the Barossa Valley or the Riverland (as it is) and is watered regularly (which it is). Now that may not sound bad, but there's no doubt that with wine grapes the higher the crops, the lower the quality. Sure, overcropped grenache can make nice rosé, and is useful in producing tanks full of cheap port, but it's not as much fun as red wine.

The trick to making a good quaffing grenache, then, is to either bring the crops down in the vineyard or blend in a little of something complementary, such as some ripe shiraz or earthy mourvèdre (a grape also known as mataro). As you can see, the latter option is the one most successfully adopted by winemakers.

This group of wines is a good demonstration of the trickle-down effect in drinking fashions. About 10 years ago, a few small premium producers like d'Arenberg in McLaren Vale and Charles Melton in the Barossa began 'rediscovering' their old, naturally low-yielding grenache vines and got rave reviews. This rekindled interest in the variety and today, many higher-volume, cheaper-priced producers have joined the renaissance. Which is a fine thing, as we reckon a good young grenache or grenache blend is possibly the best sausage wine you could find—all that spicy, earthy, sweet fruit and soft tannin…yum.

 Quaff! Award Winner   ★ Best Buy   Max's Pick   Peter's Pick

2000 Jacob's Creek Grenache Shiraz
⭐ **$8.95**

Luckily for Orlando and Jacob's Creek, the renewed interest in grenache that swelled during the 1990s coincided with a slump in interest in what used to be called 'beaujolais'—the European protected name that was used to signify light, fruity reds for early drinking. This meant that the old Jacob's Creek Beaujolais could quietly slip away into the background, to be replaced with this. The latest vintage is full of bright, sweet raspberry fruit, and has a touch of the meaty, earthy flavour grenache so often displays. Like most of the wines we recommend here, it needs to be drunk young and fresh to be appreciated fully.

1998 Leo Buring Shiraz Grenache
⭐ **$12.00**

Leo Buring is one of the most under-rated and undervalued brands in the Southcorp portfolio, but we think it deserves to be better known—and more widely drunk—for producing great quaffing wines like this one (which is sometimes discounted to under $10). It's very much a barbecue wine—especially if your barbecue is groaning with steaks—because it's fairly dark, dense and full of chewy, plummy fruit, and needs something like a good mouthful of rump to mellow it out a little.

2000 Peter Lehmann Barossa Grenache
P ⭐ **$12.00**

This deliciously light, direct and fruity young red is a great alternative to Peter Lehmann's other two Barossa reds, a shiraz and a cabernet, which are both huge, rich, oaky monsters and are both over $15 (but under $20). No, this is a much more user-friendly wine altogether (not that that the others aren't friendly—it's just that you have to be in the mood). Like pure unadulterated cherry juice with a sprinkling of peppery spice, this wine is a great example of the inherent fruit sweetness (as opposed to sugar sweetness) of the grenache grape variety. Drink with pizza.

2000 Rosemount Estate New Australian Red
⭐ **$8.95**

Another label that was brought in when the old Rosemount Beaujolais became redundant (after a few years of being labelled—rather cheekily—as BJ). This is an unusual blend of merlot, mourvèdre and grenache and is essentially an unwooded, young, light red style with heaps of vitality and quaffability. We'd never come across this combination of varieties before, but we think it works: the juicy, curranty perfume of merlot is wonderfully combined with the spice and zest of the other two grapes.

2000 Rosemount Estate Split Label Grenache Shiraz
Ⓜ ⭐ **$11.95**

The remarkable thing about this reliable everyday quaffer is the fact that it's spent some time in oak barrels—only three months, sure, but enough to give it a little more complexity, roundness and interest than you might expect at the price (regularly discounted to under $10). Oak barrels, you feel, are normally reserved for the expensive wines, aren't they? You don't notice the oak, either—it's really there just to support all the bright, ripe, red berry fruit and spicy liveliness. Very good wine, very good value.

2000 Ryecroft Flame Tree Red
⭐ **$7.95**

As with the Ryecroft Flame Tree White and the Rosemount New Australian White, there is a remarkable similarity in blend and style between this and the Rosemount New Australian Red (Ryecroft is owned by Rosemount—or, more accurately, is now a brand of Rosemount's). This, too is a blend of merlot, mourvèdre and grenache and is essentially an unwooded, young, light red style with heaps of vitality and quaffability. If anything, it's just a touch more simple, and less glowingly vibrant than its Rosemount cousin.

1999 St Hallett Gamekeepers Reserve
⭐ **$13.00**

This has been one of our favourite good value red blends for a while now, and while the price has slowly crept up, we have seen it for sale at close to $10— which makes it a bargain. One of the secrets to this wine's character-filled taste has been the use of a little touriga in the blend, along with the more usual Barossa varieties such as shiraz and grenache. Touriga is originally a Portuguese variety used for port production, but in this dry red it adds a welcome intriguing herbal spicy quality to the rich, blackcurrant jube flavours that make up most of the rest of the wine.

1997 Seaview Grenache Shiraz
⭐ $11.00

Normally we would urge you to drink wines made using grenache within the first two years or so after vintage, when all the sweet primary fruit perfumes are at their most gorgeous (most of the wines here are 1999 or 2000 vintage for a reason). But this great little cheapie shows that, thankfully, there are always exceptions to the rule. It's a deep-coloured wine, with a smoky, dense, earthy quality to the plummy dark fruit, and while not overly concentrated it does have surprising weight for the price. Good value.

1998 Wine Society Grenache Shiraz
⭐ $8.20

This big, generously flavoured red wine is almost enough reason in itself to become a member of the Wine Society. It's a blend of warmer climate Barossa grenache and cooler climate Padthaway shiraz and is an excellent example of how the two varieties are just made for each other: the firm, dark Padthaway shiraz component provides a sturdy, tannic balance to the soft, rich, ripe and black-fruity Barossa grenache. Superb value and, as we say, it's worth going through the (minor) hassle of joining to get your hands on some.
Available from the Wine Society: call 1300 723 723 or visit www.winesociety.com.au

1999 Yaldara Earth's Portrait Grenache
⭐ $9.95

Earth's Portrait is a new label from the large (and growing) Yaldara wine company, and this is possibly one of the most aptly-named wines in the book.

Grenache often has an underlying earthiness to its flavours—not earthy as in dirty, more earthy as in that lovely, sweet, wet black soil you can dig up after a rainstorm. This wine's got a little of that character, but don't worry, there's heaps of very ripe, round blackberry fruit too which should keep everybody happy. Good value.

SWEET
WINES

SWEET AND VERY SWEET WINES

In this chapter, we look at two very different kinds of sweet wines. The first, which for the sake of simplicity we've called 'sweet wines', tend to be light-bodied whites that have some residual sugar and are made to be drunk while they are young and fresh. They can be quaffed as aperitifs, or with some Asian dishes, or with light desserts such as fresh fruit salad. These can be delicious wines that unfairly attract bad press or unreasonably receive dismissive comments from wine snobs. Winemakers sometimes wonder what they have to do to tempt people to try these sweeter styles.

The second group of wines we recommend here are referred to as 'very sweet wines' and are often called 'stickies'. They are dessert wines for those who love a sweet hit at the end of a meal. The best of these produced in Australia are world-class wines that match all but the very best, made in France, Germany and Austria. The centre for the production of these outstanding Australian dessert wines is Griffith in the Riverina, which is able to make them relatively cheaply.

There may be some who question our practice of including half bottles (375ml) in our under $15 selection. We thought it fair enough as, for most people, a half bottle of dessert wine will serve as many as a full bottle of dry table wine. And we thought that you'd want to know the best stickies available in the cheaper price brackets.

 Quaff! Award Winner Best Buy Max's Pick Peter's Pick

sweet wines

2000 Brown Brothers Spatlese Lexia $12.50

Here is a leaked section of the precocious autobiography of Max Allen: 'I can't tell you how pleased I was when I found out that I liked this sweet, round fruit bomb of a wine…it's the stuff I cut my vinous teeth on'. There are few things that are more reassuring for wine writers than to find that they still admire a wine they loved in their youth. Brown Brothers have remained steadfastly on track with this popular style. Delightfully perfumed, soft, lush, and sweet on the palate with grapey flavours and a soft, gentle, sweet finish.

1996 De Bortoli Windy Peak Spatlese Riesling M $13.00

The riesling for this late-picked style was sourced from the King Valley. The fermentation was stopped while the wine still had some natural sugar (35 grams per litre) and acid was added to balance the sweetness. It has some excellent developed, toasty, limey riesling flavour with a soft, sweet finish. Max thought it was stunning.

2000 Grant Burge Lily Farm Frontignac $12.30

The white frontignac grapes for this wine came from Grant Burge's Lily Farm vineyard near Tanunda in the Barossa Valley. It is picked just before full ripeness to retain a crisp acidity and is vinified at low temperatures to retain the variety's delicate aromatics. Temperatures are lowered further still to stop fermentation at the required level of sweetness. Max enjoyed the Lily Farm's 'candied citron peel and muscat grapes' while Peter was enticed by 'its squashed mango, pawpaw and grapey flavours, lively, zesty palate and soft sweet finish.'

2000 Paul Conti 'Fronti' Late Harvest Muscat
P $14.95

This delicious fresh, light sweet white is sourced from low-yielding muscat vines on Paul and Jason Conti's Mariginyup vineyard, just north of Wanneroo on the outskirts of suburban Perth. It has a terrific reputation among locals and a few years ago won the people's choice at the Boutique Wineries Awards in Sydney. While Max commented on its 'excellent, crisp, young, muscat flavours, life and refreshing lightness', Peter couldn't resist mention of its 'glorious, grapey perfumes, fleshy texture and lingering, zingy finish'.

Renmano River Breeze Soft Sweet White
$ $4.95

This cheapie from BRL Hardys Renmark winery in the South Australian Riverland looked good in our blind tastings. It has attractive honeyed perfumes and some lemony–lime flavours, is soft, gentle and sweet and finishes with cleansing acidity. A pleasant straightforward sweetie that will appeal to many.

2000 Rosemount Traminer Riesling
$11.95

Philip Shaw has drawn on Rosemount contacts in the McLaren Vale and the Murray River Valley for the riesling and has taken the gewürztraminer from the company's Denman vineyard in the

Upper Hunter. The traminer was cold fermented to retain aromatics. About one third of the riesling was not fermented but was added to the blend as unfermented grape juice just before bottling to highlight the wine's grapey freshness. The 2000 Traminer Riesling has some floral and grapey aromas, is soft and sweet with delicate flavours and a clean, sweet finish.

1999 Sunstone Luscious Fruity White
⭐ **$7.95**

This is a surprise packet from McWilliams made from fully ripe grapes from the Riverina. It has powerful grapey aromas, is soft and lush with honey and lime flavours and a long, lingering finish with noticeable refreshing acidity. Delicious—a bargain.

very sweet wines

1999 Cranswick Estate Semillon (375ml)
⭐ **$9.99**

An appealing sticky from the Riverina which we would expect to be a crowd pleaser. Quite forward for a one-year-old sweet white but with appealing nectarine, butterscotch and passionfruit jelly flavours. It is rich, concentrated and sweet with reasonable cleansing acidity.

1996 Deen De Bortoli Vat 5 Late Harvest Semillon (375ml)
⭐ **$11.00**

This is the wine that De Bortoli refer to as the younger sister of Australia's best dessert wine, the Noble One. The Vat 5 is also sourced from the Riverina but is picked less ripe and at lower levels of botrytis infection than its more expensive sibling. It is then aged in one-year-old French barriques before bottling. Two of the four bottles that we tried were corked. With the good bottles, we appreciated the Vat 5 for its luscious toasty, honeyed characters, complexity and balance.

1997 Gramps Botrytis Semillon (375ml)
M $14.95

The Gramps Botrytis was made from semillon grown at Griffith in the Riverina and at Cowra. As with the best of these stickies, the vineyards were inspected regularly as harvest approached to ensure that the grapes were picked when ripeness, botrytis infection and sugar concentration were at their optimum. For Max, this was the best sticky: 'a sauternes style with complexity, restraint and intensity all balanced by refreshing acidity'. While Peter preferred another, he did admire the 'sweet lime juice, marmalade and apricot flavours as well as the richness and concentration of the Gramps'.

1998 John James McWilliam Late Harvest Semillon (375ml)
P $11.95

It's hard to believe but McWilliams seem to be making better stickies with each vintage. This is given luxury treatment during the production process. A portion of the juice is slow fermented at cold temperatures in tank over thirty days while the balance is fermented over three months in new and old oak barrels. The wine is then aged in old oak for twelve months before bottling. While Max was impressed, he found the JJ McWilliam 'a little over-poweringly sweet'. It was Peter's standout sticky: 'wonderfully perfumed, delicate, fresh apricot and marmalade characters'. Here is a wine that has lightness of body, lively acidity, intensity of flavour and a crisp finish that cleanses the palate.

1995 Vintage Cellars Coonawarra Botrytis Riesling (375ml)
⭐ **$10.49**

This is a find: riesling from Coonawarra is scarcely fashionable; five-year-old stickies are often past their best; and the price is amazing considering its quality and age. Forget any of your preconceptions! The wine is quite brilliant—tangy and youthful and showing some orange blossom aromas, ripe marmalade and apricot flavours, a lush texture and a delicate sweetness that is cut by zingy acidity. **Available through Vintage Cellars.**

1996 The Wine Society Botrytis Semillon (375ml)
⭐ **$11.20**

Both of us were very impressed with this cracker, made for The Wine Society by De Bortoli. It's still in great condition: ripe marmalade, lime skin and apricot flavours, soft, lush, silky texture, good richness and sweetness on the mid-palate balanced by cleansing acidity on the finish.

FORTIFIED
WINES

PORT

Throughout the first half of the twentieth century, Australia's wine industry was predominantly concerned with producing fortified wine (port and sherry), much of it for export to the UK. Table wines that we're familiar with today (crisp young riesling, bright young reds) were very much in the minority.

As a result, even though port is no longer fashionable and sales are on a steady decline, Australian winemakers are blessed with exceptional skills at making port and have good stocks of older wines maturing in the barrel—a situation which has led to some stunning bargains. There is also a strong grape resource, with grenache and shiraz (the two main grapes used for port production) often being sourced from good, mature vineyards in warm regions.

We are able to recommend a dozen ports—an excellent result, we thought, for Australia's port producers. But, to be honest, we rejected a higher number of overly sweet, dirty and stale wines which we felt didn't come up to the mark. We tended to favour those wines that had what we saw as true tawny port characters (drier, spicier, nuttier flavours imparted through long aging in small oak barrels) over those wines which were just very sweet and fortified. Having said that, if the sweet fortifieds were enjoyable drinks, we have recommended them.

And we must make mention of the very old-fashioned packaging still used by most port producers: they are clearly aiming their products at an older market, relying on past loyalty rather than trying to woo newer, younger consumers.

 Quaff! Award Winner   Best Buy   Max's Pick   Peter's Pick

highly recommended

Hardys Tall Ships Tawny Port
⭐ **$8.95**

Excellent value (you'll get sick of reading that sentiment by the end of this chapter). This is a complex, malty, treacly, soft, lush port, with good balance and an attractive nutty, spirity lift.

McWilliams Family Reserve Tawny Port
⭐ **$11.95**

From the McWilliams extensive stocks of old port maturing at their winery in Griffith, New South Wales, this is a dark, rich port with flavours of molasses and treacle, a gentle silky texture and seductive hints of spicy caramelised citrus fruit. Sensational value (see what we mean?).

Penfolds Reserve Bin 421 Tawny Port
P **$11.65**

Penfolds fortified winemaker Dean Kraehenbuhl manages to blend a lot of complexity into his wines at a great price, utilising the fantastic stocks of old port maturing in a huge warehouse at Penfolds Kalimna vineyard in the Barossa Valley. This is a less sweet style—more intense than luscious—with gentle toffee and brandy spirit aromas, soft, silky texture, with a lightness and spiciness we really liked.

Renmano Cromwell Tawny Port
⭐ **$6.95**

One of the most bizarrely named ports we tried (why you would call your wine after a seventeenth-century revolutionary is beyond us), but nevertheless one of the very best value. This had good, rich, raisiny perfumes, surprising depth of flavour and good, nutty, oak complexity.

Chateau Yaldara Liqueur Port $9.95

A good example of a youthful, light tawny port made using ripe Barossa grenache. This has glorious fresh, red-grapey smells, with spicy liveliness and a round, sweet finish. Not terribly complex or deep, it has broad appeal and is good value.

recommended

1998 d'Arenberg Vintage Shiraz 375ml $14.95

All the other wines we are recommending are tawny style ports—aged for many years in barrel, during which time the wine turns brown and picks up spicy oak flavours. This is a vintage 'port', which is quite a different style: aged in barrel for only a year or so, it is bottled while all the dark rich fruit is still present and is expected to be able to age well in the bottle for years after. This wine will age well, but we love its intense blackberry fruit and powerful, earthy flavours right now—especially if we're also tucking into some smelly blue cheese.

Hardys Whiskers Blake Tawny Port M $11.95

Unlike most of the ports we are recommending, which have been popular for decades, this brand was only introduced by Hardys a few years ago. We argued over this: Peter thought the lifted brandy spirit dominated the wine and found it too dry (as in not overly sweet); whereas Max loved it, seeing that same, spiritous character as a very good example of the traditional tawny style—more delicate and lighter, perhaps, than many other Australian ports.

Lindemans Macquarie Barossa Valley Tawny Port $11.35

Lindemans may be associated in most people's minds with the Hunter Valley, or Coonawarra, or even with huge multi-regional blends like Bin 65, but the company also has good stocks of port from the Barossa. This is a fairly complex, spicy, smoky port with smooth, rich and concentrated flavour. Good wine.

Mildara Benjamin Port $13.95

Peter liked this wine for its luscious, smooth texture, and its flavours of rich, ripe crushed raisins. Max liked it too, but thought its extreme sweetness would become a little cloying after a while. It may not be typical tawny port style and is not, perhaps, the best value wine in this bunch, but it's a fun, sweet drink.

Morris Black Label Old Tawny Port $10.95

This is great value port from one of Rutherglen's best producers. It's a very round and mellow wine, with gentle flavours of sweet raisins and toffee, made more complex by the characteristic spicy, woody flavours we associate with wines from Morris—flavours imparted over years spent in small oak barrels.

Penfolds Club Port ☆ $9.00

One of Australia's best-known and most popular ports, still packaged with a label straight out of the Menzies era, when gentlemen sipped port in the wood-panelled lounge of their club. This is a very dark, caramelly and velvety rich port with overtones of treacle and toffee, and a good, long, silky finish.

Queen Adelaide Fine Old Tawny Port
★ **$6.45**

The quality of this cheapie surprised us—for six bucks, we weren't quite expecting a complex, not-too-sweet, light and attractive port. But that's what we got: the wine has lifted, fresh, spicy spirit aromas and light, nutty, raisiny flavours on the tongue. Needless to say, great value.

cask ports

While we are happy to recommend these two casks from the ten which we tasted, ports are available for such bargain basement prices that we think you'll get much better value buying them in the bottle.

De Bortoli Premium Port (2 litres) $11.00

This is a soft, round port style which has nutty, toffee and treacle flavours and sweet, uncomplicated flavours.

Morris Oak Cask Port (2 litres) $12.95

A thick, syrupy drink with sweet, raisiny flavours, a smooth texture and some refreshing acidity.

SHERRY

It's hard to believe that sherry is so unfashionable. Things couldn't be better for those of us who love the different ways in which this delicious drop expresses itself. Australian wine companies are almost down on their knees begging consumers to buy, and try, their sherries. It's the same worldwide, even for the Spanish producers who discovered the style and gave the wine its name (a corruption of the word 'Jerez', from the city of Jerez de la Frontera in the heart of Spain's sherry producing area).

Why is sherry so untrendy? The answer is a combination of things: our love affair with table wines; random breath testing and an increased awareness of the dangers of drink driving; the demise of the business lunch; and health concerns about drinking too much—all of which has led us to being wary of the extra alcohol in fortified wines. Sales of fortified wines, which were the mainstay of the Australian wine industry until as recently as the 1970s, have dropped about 30 per cent in the past decade. As they still make up about 10 per cent of domestic consumption of wine (35 million litres in 1998), it's a significant sector of the market. And there are great bargains to be had.

It might help to understand a little about how sherry is different from table wine. The first stage in the process of making sherry involves the production of a base wine (an early picked dry white made in the usual way) to which alcohol is added. The wine is then stored in partly filled barrels which expose the wine to air, enhance oxidation and encourage the growth of the flor yeast culture which has been added to the barrels and grows like a skin on the wine's surface. At this stage the wine develops a nutty, rancio character (which means it tastes and smells of old wood)—the characteristic sherry aroma. This process takes about two months for commercial wines, although more expensive sherries can spend seven years at this stage. Next, clean alcohol spirit is added to fortify the sherry from 15–18 per cent alcohol and, finally, the sherry is aged in old oak casks for a few years before being bottled.

Mildara Chestnut Teal Oloroso Sherry
$10.95

This luscious sherry is named after the Chestnut Teal duck which is native to the Murray River, especially around the Sunraysia area of north-east Victoria. It is there that Mildara's irrigated vineyards grow the doradillo, pedro ximinez and palomino grapes from which this wine has been produced since the early 1950s. When it is fortified in the final stage of production, sweet sherry and old madeira are added to sweeten this delightful fortified before it is aged in old oak casks for about three years. There are distinctive rancio perfumes on the nose, rich mellow flavours, a smooth, lush texture and cleansing acidity on the finish. Ideal with treacle pudding or a toffee or two to finish a meal.

Mildara George Australian Sherry
$12.95

Mildara's chairman of the day, Melbourne businessman George Caro, had to follow a sugar-free diet and so was unable to enjoy winemaker Ron Haselgrove's Supreme Sherry when it made its successful debut in 1949. Consequently, one year later, ten dozen bottles of this bone dry fino style were produced as an experimental wine and named after the chairman. It is vinified from doradillo, pedro ximinez and palomino grapes grown at Sunraysia and is different from other sherry styles in that it is fermented until it is bone dry. After that it is fortified to 18 per cent with clean alcohol spirit and is aged in old oak casks for about two years. The George is soft and round with some nutty, yeasty rancio and aniseed flavours and a crisp, dry finish. Serve chilled as an aperitif—sip it and titillate your taste buds.

Mildara Supreme Dry Australian Sherry $10.95

This fino style has been produced by Mildara for just over 50 years and is sourced from pedro ximinez, palomino and doradillo grown at Sunraysia. It is produced in much the same way as the George, but, instead of being fermented until bone dry, it is left with 15 grams per litre of residual sugar, which makes it sweeter. The Supreme has toffee and marmalade aromas, quite light weight but good intensity, a silky, lush texture with some honeyed flavours and a clean, slightly sweeter finish.

Mildara Rio Vista Flor Dry Sherry $7.50

George Chaffey pioneered irrigation on the Murray River and saw the potential of the region for viticulture. His persistence in the face of overwhelming adversity laid much of the foundation for the successful development of the heartland of the Australian wine industry. This range of sherries is named after his original house at Mildura, which is now a museum.
The Rio Vista Dry Sherry has some nutty perfumes, marmalade, charry oak and nutty characters, is quite rich, well-balanced and intensely flavoured, and satisfyingly dry.

Mildara Rio Vista Medium Dry $7.50

This is a delicate fino with pale straw colour, dried apricots and rancio aromas on the nose, is clean and lively with intense, nutty flavours, a hint of sweetness and refreshing acidity on the finish.

MUSCAT AND TOKAY

If we were asked to name any wine styles which were unique to Australia, we'd mention Hunter Valley semillon, sparkling reds and fortified muscats and tokays—especially those produced from Rutherglen in north-eastern Victoria. No other country has been able to replicate these. Unfortunately, there are only a few of these quintessential Aussie fortifieds in this price bracket, so quaffers will have to look to tawny ports for a wide range of possibilities that might satisfy their desire for something with a sweet kick at the end of a meal—unless you'd like to try the four muscats that we are happy to recommend.

This is one section of the book in which we were tormented by some exquisite wines which appeared just outside our price range. The stand-out fortifieds are the Morris Liqueur Muscat and the Morris Liqueur Tokay which sell in 500ml bottles for just over $15. They are fantastic value and stunning quality, and it breaks our hearts not to be able to include them in the book. The Brown Brothers Reserve Muscat is also a little over $15 but still represents impressive value.

De Bortoli Show Liqueur Muscat
$14.50

A wonderfully good muscat: fresh and vibrant. 'Tremendously rich, syrupy and hedonistic' said Max, 'it's bound to be more than $15.' It's not, but it could be. 'Intensely grapey with an attractive sweetness that is balanced by fresh, zingy acidity and lovely lingering flavours,' said Peter.

McWilliams Family Reserve Aged Muscat
$11.95

This is an impressive fortified with deep dark, savoury flavours and a touch of fruitcake, impressive richness and concentration of flavour and a sweet, lush finish.

Morris Black Label Liqueur Muscat
$10.95

David Morris is a brilliant producer of fortified wines and this is a decent entry-level quaffer. It is splendidly fresh, has vibrant spicy grapey fruits, lush texture and a clean, soft finish.

Wandin Valley Muscat (375ml)
$13.50

This is a delightful Rutherglen muscat produced by the Hunter Valley winery of James and Philippa Davern, who happen to be Max's in-laws. 'Leave it out!' insisted Max, 'people will accuse me of favouritism!' But Peter loved its attractive, malty aromas, rich, luscious grapey flavours, fleshy texture and clean, crisp, zingy finish. So he slipped it in while Max wasn't looking.
Cellar door only: call (02) 4930 7317.

GLOSSARY

From *Red and White: wine made simple* by Max Allen, published by
New Holland Publishers.

acid   A component of grapes and wine. Despite the harsh, sour connotations of the word, acid (particularly tartaric acid) is important to the structure and balance of wine, contributing zest, life and freshness, and helping the wine age.

acidic   Zingy, crisp, fresh, lively, juicy, tangy, zesty, lemony, citrussy—these are all good synonyms for acidic when the acid has contributed positively to a wine's structure. Sharp, tart and sour can all be used to describe a wine with excessive or unbalanced acid.

aggressive   Wine that hits you in the mouth, that feels like it's marching up and down on your tongue in acid-heeled stilettos, or thumping your gums in with tannin sledgehammers, might be described as aggressive.

alcohol   Without it, wine would just be interesting grape juice. A funny poison, alcohol in moderation can be a wonderful thing; immoderation gives you a sore head and can do you serious damage.

aldehyde   A nutty-smelling compound produced when juice or wine comes into contact with oxygen in a controlled way. Most often used as a tasting adjective with styles such as sparkling and fortified, as in: 'My word, this old vintage champagne has wonderful, nutty, aldehydic characters!'

aperitif   The drink you drink before you're having a drink. Good aperitif wines, like sparkling wine or dry sherry, should tickle the tastebuds and leave you thirsty for more.

appellation Geographically defined wine region. In France, where the word originated, the 'appellation contrôlée' system is governed by detailed laws about what varieties can be planted where, and how wines can be made; in Australia, a much looser system is being developed, dealing just with the boundaries of a region. ('On this side of the road I'm standing in the Barossa Valley wine region.' Hop. 'And on this side of the road, I'm standing in the Eden Valley wine region.')

aromatic A catch-all phrase that refers to wines with strong positive aromas, such as the powerfully varietal smells of good sauvignon blanc.

austere A wine that tastes a little mean, hard and tight is austere, as though the flavours are there, but the wine doesn't want to give them to you.

autolysis Once yeast cells in bottles of sparkling wine have done their important work—causing a secondary fermentation—they die, fall to the side of the resting bottle and begin to autolyse, or decompose. After eighteen months, these autolysing cells begin to contribute a particular bready aroma to the wine, which becomes more noticeable the longer the wine spends on lees. ('My word, this late-disgorged old vintage champagne has wonderful, bready, autolytic characters!')

balanced All of life is about balance, isn't it? Wine's part of this. A wine that is balanced has all its elements—fruit, tannin, acid, length— in seamless harmony.

barrel Wooden container for maturing wine, almost always made from oak. Barrels come in many different sizes, with the barrique at 225 litres and hogshead at 300 litres being the most common in Australia, and different types of barrels give different flavours to wine matured in them. Brand-new barrels give you more oaky flavour than old barrels; smaller barrels give you more oak character than big barrels; and American barrels give you more obvious oak flavour than French barrels.

basket press An upright cylinder of vertical wooden slats, bound by metal hoops, surrounding a central screw shaft. After red wine has finished fermenting and been pumped away (the free-run wine), the remaining grape skins are shovelled inside the cylinder and heavy boards are placed on top, attached to the screw. These are then slowly turned down, and the wine that was held in the skins—rich in colour and tannins—is pressed out. Depending on the style required, this press wine or pressings is added back or left out of the free-run wine.

baumé A measure of the sugar in grapes and therefore the potential alcohol in the resultant wine. There are other measures (known as 'oechsle' or 'brix') but baumé is the most straightforward—twelve degrees baumé roughly equates to twelve per cent alcohol.

blanc de blancs Literally white wine made from white grapes, as opposed to 'blanc de noirs': white wine made from red grapes. Most often applied to sparkling wine, as in, 'My word, this blanc de blancs champagne has wonderful, lemony chardonnay characters!' or, 'My word, this blanc de noirs champagne has wonderful, strawberry pinot noir characters!'

botrytis cinerea An airborne fungus that attacks grapes in cool, humid conditions. Also known as 'noble rot', because when it infects good grape varieties such as semillon or riesling, it dehydrates the grapes, concentrating the sugar and acid substantially, and adding both glycerol (giving a luscious mouthfeel) and a particular, much-sought-after flavour to the resulting intensely sweet wine.

bottle-aged   If wines are left alone in the bottle for a number of years, they develop bottle-aged characters, quite distinct from the fresh, fruity characters they had when they were young. For most wines, this bottle age just makes them smell and taste…well, old. But some wines develop magnificent bottle-age complexity. Good dry riesling, for example, can develop a toasty and sometimes bizarre, kerosene-like aroma, and good old cabernet can develop a smell like cedar or cigar box.

buttery   Some winemaking techniques—for example, malolactic fermentation and lees contact—can contribute a rich, creamy, buttery aroma flavour to wooded whites such as chardonnay.

carbon dioxide   A by-product of fermentation, carbon dioxide is usually left to dissipate in the atmosphere, but sometimes it is intentionally captured in bottles to make sparkling wine.

carbonic maceration   Fermentation that occurs inside intact red grapes—notably the gamay grape in Beaujolais, France—producing fruity, purple-coloured wines to be drunk young.

chalky   Steely, flinty. One of many words used to describe mineral- or stone-like flavours and textures in some—especially very dry white—wines. It's perhaps too fanciful to suggest a direct link between these flavours and the mineral-rich ground the vines are grown in—but many have tried to do just that.

chaptalisation   The winemaking shortcut outlawed in Australia, of adding sugar to grape juice to increase the eventual alcohol of the wine. (Australian winemakers are allowed to add concentrated grape juice to achieve similar ends.)

chewy   Think of an aggressive wine, and tone it down a notch or two. Chewy wines (usually red) are wines with lots of grape-skin extracts such as tannin, giving a strong impression of being really thick and full in the mouth.

clean Simply, a wine that is free of faults, fresh tasting, pleasant. Clean can occasionally be a more loaded description, implying that the wine is technically correct, but not overly exciting.

closed Or dumb. You know a wine particularly well; you've tasted it quite a few times. You open a bottle and it seems but a shadow of its former self. The wine is probably a bit closed—going through a phase between primary and secondary development, or just feeling a bit reticent. Nobody knows quite why, but it does happen. The opposite, of course, is open: a wine that seems to be wearing all its flavours on its sleeve and showing off a bit.

coarse Wine that's a bit unsubtle and rough tasting is coarse—a bit too tannic, a bit too acidic. Unbalanced might be more correct; rustic might be more diplomatic.

complex You take a sniff and smell blackberries. You take another sniff and smell cherries. Another and wet undergrowth. Another and just a hint of fresh cracked pepper. You taste it and it seems to fill your mouth with a basket of dark fruits, layer upon layer coating your tongue in explosions of flavour. You're not crazy; this isn't a dream. This is a complex wine.

concentrated Seems as though the wine's flavours concentrate along the centre of your palate; often found in wines made from low yields or old vines.

decanting Pouring a wine from one vessel into another, usually to get the wine away from any sediment or crust that might have fallen to the bottom, and to allow the wine to breathe. Sediment is usually made up on tannins and pigments that, with time, have fallen out of solution (in red wine) and tartrate crystals, the solidified form of tartaric acid (in both red and white). Breathing gets rid of any bottle stink or stale odours that may have built up over time, too, and perks the wine up a bit by giving it a gentle shake.

dusty   The tannins in young red wines give a bizarre impression of being dry and dusty along the sides and back of your tongue.

earthy   A whole spectrum of aromas and smells fall under this word. Italian reds and older reds from quite a few places often leave a really strong impression of actually having wet clay, forest floor or sweet soil in the bottle. A good thing, too—earthy wines can be delicious.

extractive   A red wine which has a little too much colour and/or tannin for its own good, so is unbalanced.

fat   Self-explanatory, really: a wine that fills the mouth and sits like a lump on the palate. Not necessarily a good thing, as it indicates the wine doesn't have enough acidity to balance it up.

faults   Things can, and occasionally do, go wrong with wine at any stage from when the grapes are picked to when the bottle is opened. Whether because of the avoidable, like too much sulphur dioxide being added by the winemaker, or the unavoidable, like a tainted cork, the things listed below indicate faults in wine. If you find them in your wine, you have every right to complain, send back the bottle to the waiter, or ask for an exchange from the bottle shop.

fault 1:   **hazy appearance** In some wines (pinot noir labelled as 'unfiltered', for example), cloudiness is perfectly okay, but in wines that should be crystal clear—a one-year-old riesling, for example—it can indicate bacterial spoilage.

fault 2: **wrong colour** Remember that brown is the colour of age, so if you open that one-year-old riesling—a wine that should be sunlight-bright, with flashes of green—and it's a dull ochre, this probably means the wine has oxidised (has reacted with oxygen and is on its way to becoming vinegar). While we're on appearance, it's worth mentioning that glass-like crystals in older white wine, and dark crunchy bits in older red wine are not faults, but natural deposits that can occur with age.

fault 3: **aldehydic smells** Unless, of course, you're smelling a wine that is meant to be aldehydic (like some fortifieds), these smells are usually unwanted and indicate the wine has oxidised. Again, if our young riesling smells like a dry sherry it's definitely faulty.

fault 4: **rotten eggs** This particularly pungent smell comes from hydrogen sulphide, which can form in a wine during fermentation. It is usually easily dealt with by the winemaker, but occasionally creeps into the bottle. Over time, it can form mercaptans, compounds that smell like burnt rubber or boiled vegies. Not to be confused with excessive sulphur dioxide, which can smell like burnt matches, and can also be a fault.

fault 5: **vinegary or solvent smells** These come from excessive levels of volatile acidity (known as VA), and/or ethyl acetate. The volatile acids (such as the vinegar acid, acetic acid) are the ones we can smell. Ethyl acetate is formed when acetic acid combines with alcohol. A little VA can add complexity and lift the aromas of a wine; a lot can make it smell like paint stripper.

fault 6: **musty, mouldy smells** These can occasionally be caused by the wine being stored in dirty, old barrels but most often a musty smell is caused by the grandpappy of all wine faults: cork taint. When you think about it, the idea that wine costing sometimes hundreds of dollars a bottle is stoppered with a bit of old bark is quite odd, to say the least. That little cylinder of bark, stripped from a tree in Portugal, although boiled and sterilised, is full of tiny holes and prone to all kinds of contamination—even, perversely, contamination from the very bleach used to sterilise it! Bad cork taint, or corkiness, manifests itself as a really rank, mouldy smell and taste, but it can, at very low levels, merely dull the wine and make it taste a little flat. Estimates of how much wine is affected run between two and twelve per cent of all bottles. Many producers are experimenting with new ways to close the bottle: synthetic corks, plastic seals, even crown seals like you'd find on a beer bottle.

When they are present in excessive amounts, all these faults are pretty easy to spot. But, of course, they are rarely present in excessive amounts, and different people have different sensitivities to the various faults. For instance, I need a wine to have really obvious volatile acidity (VA) to be put off by it, whereas the person sitting next to me might be screwing up their nose at the merest hint of VA. On the other hand, I smell cork taint at a hundred paces, when everybody else has almost finished the bottle and is saying how much they enjoyed it. Remember also that one person's minor fault may be somebody else's distinctive and appealing character.

fermentation　The furious, frenzied, bubbling process where yeasts convert sugar to alcohol, carbon dioxide and heat.

fining and filtering　People like to drink wine that is crystal clear and bright. This can be achieved by racking (pumping the wine off its lees) and allowing it to settle, but there is a small risk of minute bacteria and even yeasts making their way into the bottle during this process, making it hazy and causing all sorts of problems. So the vast majority of winemakers also fine and filter. Fining is the process of adding an agent such as egg white (very traditional) or bentonite clay (more modern) to pull the tiny particles out of the wine and clarify it. Filtering is done by passing the wine through a very fine filter. Purists claim that these processes also strip the wine of some of its flavour and character, so they don't fine or filter their wine, preferring complexity to stability.

firm Solid, taut, tense, sturdy—a more pleasant version of austere.

fleshy A more positive way of saying 'fat': a wine with plenty of palpable fruit in the mouth.

floral Literally, smelling of flowers.

forward A wine that seems to be getting old before its time.

fragrant A wine with lifted, sometimes ethereal, light, delicate aromas.

fruity Literally, smelling strongly of fruit. But which fruit? Some grape varieties have distinctive fruit aromas associated with them—the lychees of gewurztraminer, the blackcurrant of cabernet sauvignon, for example. Some wines, expecially blends of more than one grape variety, just smell broadly of 'red fruits' or 'citrus fruits'.

full-bodied A wine that fills the mouth and seems to impose on the palate—in contrast with medium- and light-bodied wines, which make a less imposing impression.

gamey Similar territory to the earthy range of smells; gamey, leathery, meaty smells and flavours often appear in older red wines.

grapey   Seems obvious, doesn't it? But very few wines actually smell like grapes, with wines made from the muscat grape being a notable exception.

herbaceous   There are two main reasons why a wine might smell grassy, herbaceous or green. It's either meant to—like sauvignon blanc—or the grapes that made it were under-ripe—like some red wines grown in very cool climates.

honeyed   Wine showing a strong smell of honey; usually associated with older whites, especially wooded dry wines such as chardonnay, and sweeter, botrytis-affected wines.

hot   Wine made from overripe grapes grown in warm climates can produce a hot-tasting burn of alcohol at the back of the throat. The fruit in those wines can also taste a bit jammy.

lees   All the crap that falls to the bottom of a tank, barrel or vat of fermenting wine—the dead yeast cells, the bits of pulp, the seeds and some bits of skin and stalk. Also refers to the dead yeast cells that fall to the bottom of a bottle of sparkling wine after its secondary fermentation.

lifted   Sometimes the delicate, spicy or fragrant aromas in a wine seem to be lifted towards your nose by some invisible hand. This is often volatile acidity, in its restrained and benevolent form, adding a little piquancy to the aroma.

long   A very good thing. A wine that has a long finish is one whose flavours seem to go on and on and on for seconds, right down the back of your throat. The opposite, obviously, is a wine with a short finish, which is nowhere near as enjoyable.

malolactic fermentation   The process that can take place in newly fermented wine where very crisp, hard malic acid (the acid found in tart apples) is converted by bacteria to much softer, lactic acid (the acid found in milk). It can happen spontaneously, but most winemakers induce it.

mildew and other diseases There are a number of diseases that the grape vine can fall prey to. The most common in Australia are the mildews (powdery and downy), which attack vines, and the rots (notably *Botrytis cinerea*), which attack grapes. These diseases occur in humid weather, and can have harmful effects on the yield and the health of the vine.

mousse The mousse is to sparkling wine what the head is to beer. A good sparkling wine should have a mousse that remains in the glass for the duration of the drink, and the bubbles that form it (called the bead) should be as small as possible. As in: 'My word, this young non-vintage champagne has a wonderful, persistent mousse and terribly fine bead!'

must After the grapes have been crushed, and before they become wine, the juice, pulp, skins and other goodies are knows as 'must'.

nutty Sometimes it's because of the barrels they're stored in (chardonnay), and sometimes it's a character of the variety they're made from (pinot gris), but flavours of nuts—hazel, brazil, almond, you name it—can crop up in white wines when you least expect them.

oily Very rarely encountered, so don't worry about it too much, but occasionally, white wines—like those made from viognier or marsanne—can have a really slippery, oily texture to them that isn't at all unattractive.

oxidation You know when you cut open an apple or an eggplant and before your eyes the exposed surface goes brown? That's oxidation—the effect of oxygen on the chemicals in the food. Oxygen can have the same effect on wine; the wine slowly oxidises and goes brown and flat, eventually turning into vinegar. But in a controlled way—in the production of sherry and some sparkling wine, for example—exposure to oxygen can make the wine more complex.

phylloxera A tiny, incredibly hard-to-eradicate louse that likes to munch on the roots of grapevines (which steadily decreases the yield of the vine and eventually kills it). Phylloxera swept through Europe and much of Australia at the end of the nineteenth century, devouring vineyards as it went. Then it was discovered that American vines were immune to the louse, so now most vineyards in phylloxera-prone areas (and that means just about anywhere) are planted on American rootstocks. Phylloxera is still there, though, and ungrafted vineyards—apart from those planted in sandy soil (a habitat the louse isn't fond of)—are still at risk.

pungent More than just aromatic, pungent refers to those special moments when you come across a wine that really lets off a smell—mostly good, but sometimes not. Really good gewürztraminer and sauvignon blanc can be pungent.

rancio A quite off-putting tasting term that refers to the quite delicious roasted nuts and bitter caramel smell of some very old and lovely fortified wines.

reserve Strictly should mean wine held in reserve to be released at a later date, but is used in Australia as a general indication of better-than-average quality—as are 'show reserve', 'winemaker's selection', and so on. Real reserve wines (wines reserved from previous vintages) are very important as blending components in sparkling wine production.

rich Wine with lots of viscosity, flesh, substance and fruit.

smoky Some white varieties such as gewürztraminer and pinot gris can make wines with a dusky, smoky perfume; and sometimes barrels can give wine that's stored in them a different, more pungent, smoky, charred, aroma.

soft Docile, smooth, elegant, well-balanced, mature, approachable—all different ways of saying delicious.

spicy Like smoky aromas, spicy characters can come from the grape varieties—the pepperiness of shiraz, for example—or the barrel—the clove and aniseed aromas of some (French) oak.

spritzig A fine fizz in the glass and a gentle prickle on the tongue indicating that small amounts of carbon dioxide were dissolved in the wine when it was bottled.

stalky A little stalkiness (in wines that have been fermented with a few of the grape stems included) can be a good, complex thing. A lot just makes a wine taste green and stalky.

sulphur Sulphur has been used as a winemaking additive to prevent oxidation for thousands of years. Sulphur candles used to be burned inside barrels to build up a layer of sulphur dioxide. Now, sulphur dioxide is added to the wine in powdered form. Another sulphur compound, copper sulphate, is used in the vineyard against mildew in the form of Bordeaux mixture, the characteristic blue spray used by many gardeners on fruit trees.

tannin Make yourself a nice pot of tea. Let it stew until it's cold and almost black, then pour a cup, and don't add anything to it. Now take a sip. It will taste disgusting, but more importantly, you'll feel like your gums and the sides of your mouth are being sucked through the taste buds on your tongue. This puckering astringency is caused by the tannins in the tea—and these tannins are also found in grape skins and stalks. Red wines are usually high in tannin (described as being very tannic) if they are made from grapes with thick skins, or have had extensive maceration or some contact with stalks during fermentation. Tannins can also leach out of oak barrels into the wine stored in them.

terroir How the unique combination of soil, slope, sunlight, and so on in a vineyard affects the taste of the resulting wine. For the French, the idea of terroir is traditional and sacrosanct ('This wine tastes of its terroir'). New World winemakers, on the other hand, are only slowly coming to terms with the concept.

thin The opposite of fat, and hardly ever a good thing. Thin wines, wines that are really neutral-tasting, that seem hollow and lean, are usually the result of overcropped grapes and poor winemaking.

ullage Given the chance, wine likes to evaporate if it's kept hanging around. It will evaporate through the cracks and loosely sealed bungs of a barrel, and it will leak and evaporate through a contracting and expanding cork in a bottle. The space that's left in the barrel and the bottle is called the ullage. Barrels can be topped up, as can very old, precious bottles—by having their corks taken out and the space filled with a younger vintage of the same wine. But most bottles are left to ullage away over the years. Badly ullaged wines, whose levels have fallen below the shoulder of the bottle, tend to oxidise as well, but a little ullage is not necessarily so harmful.

variety/varietal Two words which are often confused. A grape variety is a type of grape. A varietal wine is a wine made from one variety. (Varietal is also used as a tasting term to describe a wine that smells and tastes varietally correct—blackcurrant cabernet, for example; or peppery shiraz).

velvety   Wine which is seamless, balanced and has a smooth, supple texture in the mouth. Often applied to good pinot noir.

vinous   Just like the word grapey, you'd think a word that means 'wine-like' would crop up more often in wine tasting, wouldn't you? Funnily enough, it's hardly ever used.

viticulture   The practice of growing vines—in this case, the grapevine, and in particular, the wine grapevine, *Vitis vinifera*. People who do it are called 'viticulturists'. As the wine world looks harder at growing better grapes, 'viticulturists' are a crop of specialists you may well hear more about.

woody   Again, a catch-all term that covers all sorts of descriptions from the vanilla-like smell of new oak barrels to the cedarwood smell of old cabernet, and also covering the toasty smells, the spicy smells, the dusty smells and even the dirty old barrel smells.

yeast   There are micro-organisms and there are micro-organisms. Amoeba, for example, aren't much fun on the whole. But yeast—ah, there's a different culture of cells altogether. Yeast is the key that unlocks the intoxicating secret of the sugar in grape juice—it's the yeast cells, already in the air or introduced by the winemaker, that convert that sugar into alcohol, carbon dioxide and heat. Without yeast, wine wouldn't be nearly as much fun.

tasting notes